The Low Calorie Menu Book

A magazine just for slimmers? It would never work. At least that's what Audrey Eyton and her partner were told when they founded *Slimming Magazine* twelve years ago. The first magazine in the world expressly designed for the weight-conscious, it was an instant success with the thousands of men and women valiantly trying to eat their celery and carrot sticks in a world where everyone else seemed to be living on cream buns. Today *Slimming Magazine* is one of the most popular magazines Britain has ever seen.

Audrey Eyton edited the magazine herself for many years and later became its Editorial Director. During those years she and her partner also started Ragdale Hall Health Farm, as well as founding and developing one of Britain's largest chains of slimming clubs.

Audrey Eyton has worked with most of the world's leading nutritional, medical and psychological experts and has acquired an extensive knowledge and understanding of her subject.

Joyce Hughes is a freelance journalist and well-known writer on slimming and cookery, as well as a

Other books LOW CA MING COOKB ZINE'S QUICK also available from Arrow books.

The Low Calorie Menu Book

Joyce Hughes
and Audrey Eyton

Slimming Magazine *Handbooks* No. 1

ARROW BOOKS

Arrow Books Limited
17–21 Conway Street, London W1P 6JD

An imprint of the Hutchinson Publishing Group

London Melbourne Sydney Auckland
Johannesburg and agencies
throughout the world

First published 1980
Reprinted 1982

© Slimming Magazine 1980

Made and printed in Great Britain
by The Anchor Press Ltd
Tiptree, Essex

ISBN 0 09 922640 5

—Contents—

—Introduction—

On 1000 calories a day your weight *will* melt away. And that's a promise! Here is a book of 1000-calorie menus designed to give you maximum choice and flexibility in keeping your daily calorie intake to that magic 1000! It has been devised by the nutritionists of *Slimming* magazine, using all the expertise of the world's leading publication on the subject.

Why can *Slimming* magazine be so confident that you can shed all those surplus pounds by keeping to the menus in this book? Because the average woman uses up at least 2000 calories a day in keeping her body 'ticking over' and in moving around. The average man uses considerably more calories. So if you only eat 1000 calories a day those extra 1000 or more calories you "spend" have got to come from somewhere. And the only place they can come from is your store of surplus fat. That's what slimming is all about!

Some women suspect that they can't shed weight on 1000 calories a day but when this has been put to the test by feeding them in can't-make-a-mistake conditions (*Slimming* magazine have performed such tests them-

selves in their own Slimming Hydro, Ragdale Hall) they
have almost invariably lost weight. The problem lay in
their own errors in measuring out their daily 1000
calories worth of food.

Most women, in fact, could shed weight on a more
generous allowance of 1500 calories a day. Only those
who are experiencing a metabolic slow-down after long
months of dieting, or only have a few surplus pounds to
shed, are likely to have to restrict themselves to a precise
1000 calories a day.

However, for all slimmers there can be certain advan-
tages in aiming for that 1000 calorie a day maximum.

The main advantage, of course, is speed of weight loss.
We often suspect that slimming advisers who preach 'be
content with a half pound weight loss each week, do it
slowly' have never had to do the wretched thing themselves. Slimming is a bore. We can only promise to make
it *less* difficult, *less* sacrificial, and easi*er*. We would be
the last people to claim that dieting is easy. Still less –
Heaven forbid – would we go around claiming that
'slimming is fun'. What rubbish!

The only joy of slimming – and it is an *enormous* joy
which makes all the effort worthwhile – is the pure
unadulterated pleasure of looking at the scales and
receiving visual proof that another couple of those
wretched pounds have 'bitten the dust'. Life holds few
moments of joy and satisfaction that can compare with
the discovery that you have achieved another good
weekly weight loss.

People who don't achieve a weight loss speedy and
satisfying enough to keep up their morale usually give up
dieting completely. So reasonably speedy results are very
important.

On a 1000-calorie diet most women could expect to
achieve a reasonably speedy weight loss in the region of at
least 2 lbs per week. But accuracy is needed to keep to this
calorie intake. Remember that on low calorie diets like

this all foods have to be weighed and measured. Remember that little morsels of this and that, the butter you spread but didn't measure, the milk you poured in your coffee but didn't calorie-count, can quickly add hundreds of extra calories to your daily intake. And remember that 'eating amnesia' is a very common problem among dieters!

What is the best way in which to eat your 1000 calories a day?

There is only one answer to that question. That is: 'the way which is easiest for you'. And your answer will be a very individual one; there is no one type of dieting menu which is easiest for everyone.

Some people will find it easier to keep to their daily calorie ration if they divide it into lots of little snacks; others will find it easier if they save most of their calories for two good meals; some will only find it possible to keep to their allowance if they are allowed to include some alcohol or 'a little of what they fancy' in the way of sugary or starchy snacks. There are endless variations.

In this book of ready-planned 1000-calorie menus you will find some of the most useful variations. Choose the menus which best suit your requirements, or experiment to discover which are easiest for you, or switch around, to suit the day and the occasion.

All that matters is that you keep on eating only 1000 calories a day for as long as it takes. In which case you will get slim. As we said, that's a promise!

–Little-and-Often–
Menus

The 1000-calorie menus in this chapter are designed for dieters who find it difficult to keep to three meals a day, hard to resist between-meal snacks. If you describe yourself as an 'inveterate nibbler', these are the ideal diet menus for you.

Here your daily 1000 calories are divided into four, five or six little snacks, which means no big meals – but also no big gaps between meals.

Slimming *magazine* has found this multi-meal method of dieting to be one of the most successful they have ever devised. By catering to those compulsive eating urges, which can arise mid-morning, during the evening, at any time of day irrespective of what you might have eaten at a previous meal, this diet method has made it possible for *many women to keep to their correct daily slimming calorie allowance for the first time.*

The slimmer who follows this little-and-often pattern of eating also achieves a useful advantage in speed of weight loss. Because the metabolic rate, the rate at which your body burns up fat, increases a little after a meal, little-and-often dieting means that you are burning up fat slightly faster throughout most hours of the day. The speed advantage is just a small one, but a useful bonus for those who also find this method the easiest to follow.

No one has the time to cook elaborate dishes five or six times a day, so you will find that all the little meals and snacks in this section are very simple and easy to prepare.

Menu No. 1

Drinks allowance:

275ml/½ pint silver-top milk allowed for sugarless tea or coffee throughout the day. Unlimited low-calorie drinks and water.

Meal 1

2 rashers streaky bacon, well-grilled
45ml/3 tablespoons canned tomatoes
1 slice slimmers' bread, unbuttered

Meal 2

25g/1oz slice of bread, toasted and topped with 25g/1oz grated
Edam cheese

Meal 3

170g/6oz packet of Findus cod in parsley sauce
50g/2oz boiled peas
1 tomato

Meal 4
1 McVitie's chocolate digestive biscuit
1 orange

Meal 5
1 egg (size 2), boiled
15g/½oz grated cheese
15ml/1 tablespoon low-calorie salad dressing
mixed salad

Grill bacon, sausages and chops really crisp to shed those fatty calories.

Menu No. 2

Drinks allowance:
275ml/½ pint silver-top milk allowed for sugarless tea or coffee throughout the day. Unlimited low-calorie drinks and water.

Meal 1
141g/5oz carton low-fat natural yogurt
1 orange

Meal 2
1 small packet KP Cheesey Crunchies

Meal 3
2 frozen fish cakes, grilled without fat
125g/4oz baked beans

Meal 4

2 crispbreads spread with 15g/½oz beef paste or sardine and
tomato paste, topped with 1 tomato, sliced

Meal 5

227g/8oz packet Birds Eye shepherd's pie
75g/3oz carrots
50g/2oz boiled green beans

—— *Menu No. 3* ——

Drinks allowance:

275ml/½ pint silver-top milk allowed for sugarless tea or
coffee throughout the day. Unlimited low-calorie drinks
and water.

Meal 1

1 egg (size 4), poached
170g/6oz pack Findus smoked Scottish haddock, buttered

Meal 2

2 cream crackers with 15g/½oz portion cheese spread

Meal 3

2 frozen beefburgers, well-grilled, served with 75g/3oz boiled
green beans, and 1 grilled tomato

Meal 4

1 Wall's Golden Vanilla Choc Ice bar

Meal 5

1 can Heinz low-calorie chicken with vegetable soup
1 crispbread with a little low-fat spread

Menu No. 4

Drinks allowance:
275ml/½ pint silver-top milk allowed for sugarless tea or coffee throughout the day. Unlimited slimmers' low-calorie drinks and water.

Meal 1
½ grapefruit
1 egg (size 4), poached on 1 slice slimmers' bread, toasted

Meal 2
Sandwich made from 2 slices slimmers' bread with 7g/¼oz low-fat spread such as Outline and 40g/1½oz liver sausage and watercress

Meal 3
1 Ski fruit yogurt

Meal 4
50g/2oz shelled prawns or shrimps with a salad of lettuce, cucumber and watercress
15ml/1 tablespoon Waistline seafood sauce

Meal 5
1 small packet Smith's crisps
25g/1oz Edam cheese

Solemnly swear to weigh all food portions until you are absolutely sure that you know what each portion you serve yourself looks like. Carelessness over the size of portion you help yourself to can slow your slimming considerably.

————*Menu No. 5*————

Drinks allowance:

275ml/½ pint silver-top milk *or* 550ml/1 pint skimmed or separated milk allowed for sugarless drinks throughout the day. Unlimited low-calorie drinks and water.

Meal 1

1 egg (size 5) mixed with 15ml/1 tablespoon milk from drinks allowance and scrambled in non-stick pan using 3g/⅛oz low-fat spread
1 slice slimmers' bread, plain or toasted

Meal 2

Peel, core and slice a 175g/6oz cooking apple. Stew with 5ml/1 teaspoon water and 5ml/1 teaspoon sugar. Add a pinch of cinnamon and turn into a small dish. Sprinkle with 15g/½oz 30% Bran Flakes just before serving

Meal 3

2 frozen beefburgers, well grilled
15ml/1 tablespoon tomato sauce
1 grilled tomato
75g/3oz boiled green beans

Meal 4

25g/1oz slice wholemeal bread, lightly buttered
25g/1oz peeled prawns mixed with 10ml/2 teaspoons low-calorie seafood sauce

Meal 5

1 chicken drumstick (100g/3½oz raw weight) grilled
mixed salad of lettuce, cucumber, spring onions
15ml/1 tablespoon low-calorie cream-type salad dressing
1 orange

—————*Menu No. 6*—————

Drinks allowance:
This menu gives you 4 meals and allows 3 glasses of wine.
Tea and coffee *without* milk allowed.

Meal 1

1 lamb's kidney, grilled
1 average rasher of back bacon, well-grilled
1 grilled tomato
1 slice of slimmers' bread spread with 3g/⅛oz butter

Meal 2

170g/6oz packet Birds Eye cod in shrimp-flavoured sauce
30ml/2 tablespoons green beans

Meal 3

2 slices slimmers' bread spread with 7g/¼oz butter and filled
with 40g/1½oz corned beef

Meal 4

75g/3oz roast chicken
30ml/2 tablespoons gravy, made without fat
125g/4oz mixed vegetables

Meal 5(!)

3 glasses (115ml/4fl.oz each) dry white wine

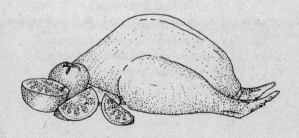

————Menu No. 7————

Drinks allowance:
Unlimited tea with lemon only, black coffee and low-calorie drinks. No milk allowed for drinks.

Breakfast
125ml/4 fl. oz natural orange juice
1 egg (size 4), boiled
1 Ryvita crispbread spread with 3g/⅛oz butter

Mid-morning
2 rich tea biscuits with black coffee

Lunch
large plate of salad vegetables (mushrooms, tomato, lettuce, watercress, celery, cucumber, green pepper, grated carrot)
15ml/1 tablespoon low-calorie salad dressing such as Waistline
50g/2oz prawns

Afternoon break
2 fingers Kit-Kat

Children's tea-time
1 apple

Dinner
275g/10oz chicken joint, roasted or baked
1 ring canned pineapple, drained
75g/3oz cooked portion of Birds Eye savoury vegetable rice
(peas, rice and mushrooms)
1 Ryvita crispbread spread with 1 portion Kraft Dairylea cheese
spread

Late evening (supper)
1 can Heinz low-calorie oxtail soup

Menu No. 8

Drinks allowance:

As much tea without milk and black coffee and as many low-calorie drinks as you wish.

Meal 1

150ml/5 fl. oz low-fat natural yogurt
1 medium-size 175g/6oz banana

Meal 2

3 fish fingers, grilled without fat
2 grilled tomatoes
1 tablespoon of boiled peas
1 apple

Meal 3

213g/7½oz can Crosse and Blackwell spaghetti rings with tomato sauce served on 2 slices slimmers' bread, toasted (no butter)

Meal 4

1 sachet Cadbury's beef and tomato snacksoup
2 Ryvita spread with 7g/¼oz butter and filled with 25g/1oz grated Edam cheese and 1 sliced tomato

Meal 5

1 Penguin biscuit
milky coffee made with 150ml/¼pint low-fat skimmed milk

Menu No. 9

Drinks allowance:

275ml/½ pint silver-top milk for drinks throughout the day. As much sugarless tea and coffee and as many low-calorie drinks as you wish.

Meal 1

1 egg (size 4), poached and served on a slice of slimmers' bread, toasted

Meal 2

2 Ryvita spread with 7g/¼oz butter
25g/1oz lean ham
a sliced tomato

Meal 3

142g/5oz packet Birds Eye liver with onion and gravy
75g/3oz boiled carrots

Meal 4

113g/4oz Eden Vale cottage cheese
1 stick of celery

Meal 5

206g/7oz can Heinz spaghetti bolognese (without toast please)

Weigh out 25g/1oz butter or low-fat spread such as Outline or Gold taken straight from the fridge. Then cut it into 4 or 8 pieces, according to whether you are allowed 3g/⅛oz or 7g/¼oz, ready to use for spreading or cooking when allowed. This way you eliminate the guesswork.

—————*Menu No. 10*—————

Drinks allowance:

275ml/½pint silver-top milk for drinks throughout the day. As much sugarless tea and coffee and as many low-calorie drinks as you wish.

Meal 1

1 egg (size 4), boiled
1 crispbread, lightly buttered

Meal 2

25g/1oz Edam cheese
1 apple

Meal 3

175g/6oz fillet of white fish grilled or steamed
75g/3oz boiled peas
1 grilled tomato
50g/2oz mushrooms stewed in stock

Meal 4

1 average-sized banana

Meal 5

142g/5oz pack Birds Eye braised kidneys in gravy
125g/4oz boiled carrots
125g/4oz boiled Brussels sprouts

Meal 6

2 crispbreads
15g/½oz portion cheese spread

—————— *Menu No. 11*——————

Drinks allowance:

275ml/½ pint low-fat skimmed milk for drinks throughout the day. As much tea and coffee and as many low-calorie drinks as you wish.

Meal 1

2 rashers streaky bacon, well grilled
1 slice of slimmers' bread
5ml/1 teaspoon tomato sauce

Meal 2

1 carton low-fat natural yogurt
1 apple or orange

Meal 3

3 fish fingers, grilled without fat
75g/3oz green beans
1 grilled tomato

Meal 4

113g/4oz carton cottage cheese
large mixed salad (no dressing)

Meal 5

125g/4oz lamb's liver, braised in Oxo stock with a small onion, chopped
75g/3oz boiled carrots
125g/4oz boiled cabbage

Meal 6

1 can Heinz low-calorie chicken or mushroom soup

Menu No. 12

Drinks allowance:
As much sugarless tea and coffee without milk and as many low-calorie drinks as you wish.

Meal 1
20g/¾oz Rice Krispies
65ml/⅛ pint silver-top milk
5ml/1 level teaspoon sugar

Meal 2
1 Penguin biscuit

Meal 3
170g/6oz packet Birds Eye chicken and mushroom casserole
75g/3oz boiled carrots
125g/4oz green grapes

Meal 4
2 Ry-King Slim Light crispbreads
25g/1oz Edam cheese

Meal 5
175g/6oz grilled white fish brushed with 3g/⅛oz butter
50g/2oz sweetcorn
2 grilled tomatoes

Meal 6
Small packet of Golden Wonder crisps

Menu No. 13

Drinks allowance:

275ml/½ pint silver-top *or* 550ml/1 pint skimmed or separated milk allowed for sugarless drinks throughout the day.

Meal 1

25g/1oz 30% Bran Flakes
75ml/3 fl. oz milk (extra to allowance)
5ml/1 level teaspoon sugar

Meal 2

150ml/5 fl. oz low-fat natural yogurt with 6 dried apricots, chopped, and 15ml/1 tablespoon orange juice

Meal 3

170g/6oz packet Findus cod steak in cheese or parsley or butter sauce
125g/4oz boiled green beans

Meal 4

2 large tomatoes, hollowed and stuffed with 50g/2oz cottage cheese mixed with 25g/1oz lean ham, diced

Meal 5

1 slice slimmers' bread, toasted, with a scraping of low-fat spread and topped with 25g/1oz liver sausage and 1 stuffed olive, sliced

Menu No. 14

Drinks allowance:
275ml/½ pint silver-top milk *or* 550ml/1 pint skimmed or separated milk allowed for sugarless drinks throughout the day.

Meal 1
½ grapefruit
1 egg (size 5), boiled
slice slimmers' bread with a scraping of low-fat spread

Meal 2
150g/5oz baked beans
slice slimmers' bread, toasted with a scraping of low-fat spread
1 apple

Meal 3
1 lamb's kidney, grilled
1 rasher back bacon, well-grilled
1 grilled tomato
50g/2oz mushrooms, poached in water

Meal 4
2 fresh or canned peach halves, filled with 50g/2oz cottage cheese with pineapple mixed with 25g/1oz lean ham, chopped

Meal 5
200ml/7 fl. oz milk (extra to allowance), heated and served with 10ml/2 heaped teaspoons drinking chocolate

-No-Fuss Menus-

Many dieters want to spend as little time as possible in the kitchen while they are dieting. The menus in this chapter are designed for them.

They offer you simple meals like easy grills. They make full use of those instant frozen meals, on sale in every grocery shop, which are such a boon for slimmers. Many of these frozen meals are low in calories, and by using them you not only cut out the fuss of cooking, but the fuss of weighing and measuring too.

Here are some ideal 1000-calorie menus for busy days.

Menu No. 1

Drinks allowance:
275ml/½ pint silver-top milk for use in sugarless tea and coffee. Unlimited water or slimmers' low-calorie drinks.

Breakfast
bacon sandwich made from 2 rashers streaky bacon, well-grilled, 15ml/1 tablespoon tomato sauce and 2 slices slimmers' bread (unbuttered)

Lunch
75g/3oz corned beef
½ × 227g/8oz carton Matteson's coleslaw in vinaigrette
1 tomato and a few lettuce leaves

Evening meal
1 pack Findus beef curry

Menu No. 2

Drinks allowance:
275ml/½ pint low-fat skimmed milk and as much sugarless tea and coffee as you like; also unlimited water and slimmers' low-calorie drinks.

Breakfast
½ grapefruit
1 rasher streaky bacon, well-grilled
1 grilled tomato
2 lamb's kidneys, lightly oiled and grilled

Lunch

75g/3oz sliced cold roast beef
mixed salad of lettuce, cucumber, watercress and tomato
15ml/1 tablespoon low-calorie salad dressing
1 slice slimmers' bread, lightly spread with low-fat spread
1 medium-sized banana

Evening meal

1 pack Birds Eye chicken and mushroom casserole
25g/1oz long-grain rice, boiled
75g/3oz frozen mixed vegetables, boiled
1 crispbread
15g/½oz portion cheese spread

Menu No. 3

Drinks allowance:

275ml/½ pint low-fat skimmed milk and as much sugar-less tea and coffee as you like; also unlimited water and slimmers' low-calorie drinks.

Breakfast

150ml/¼ pint natural orange or grapefruit juice
175g/6oz fillet smoked haddock, grilled with 7g/¼oz butter
1 slice slimmers' bread (unbuttered)

Lunch

1 pack Birds Eye liver with onion and gravy
50g/2oz peas
50g/2oz mushrooms poached in stock or water
150g/5 fl. oz carton Ski yogurt

Evening meal

1 egg (size 5), hard boiled
50g/2oz prawns
15ml/1 tablespoon low-calorie salad dressing
mixed salad of lettuce, cucumber, watercress, green pepper,
tomato and spring onion
1 apple

——————Menu No. 4——————

Drinks allowance:

Unlimited sugarless tea and coffee with 185ml/⅓ pint of
silver-top milk *or* 275ml/½ pint skimmed milk and as
many low-calorie drinks as you wish.

Breakfast

½ grapefruit
2 rashers streaky bacon, *well*-grilled
1 egg (size 5), fried

Lunch

170g/6oz packet of Birds Eye cod in shrimp-flavoured sauce
125g/4oz runner beans
1 orange

Evening meal

150g/5oz lamb loin chop, well-grilled
1 lamb's kidney, grilled
50g/2oz peas
2 grilled tomatoes
141g/5oz carton St Ivel or Farmer's Wife low-fat natural yogurt
1 apple

Menu No. 5

Drinks allowance:

Unlimited sugarless black coffee and lemon tea, also slimmers' low-calorie drinks and water.

Breakfast

150ml/¼ pint natural orange juice
25g/1oz All Bran
5ml/1 teaspoon sugar
65ml/2½ fl. oz silver-top milk

Lunch

1 frozen beefburger, grilled and placed on 1 slice of toast from a
large thin sliced loaf and topped with 25g/1oz grated Cheddar
cheese and 10ml (1 dessertspoon) sweet pickle
2 grilled tomatoes

Evening meal

283g/10oz can Heinz low-calorie beef and mushroom or
tomato or chicken and vegetable soup
2 Findus cheese and ham pancakes fried as directed
100g/4oz canned butter beans
100g/4oz boiled or canned carrots
1 pear

Menu No. 6

Drinks allowance:

275ml/½ pint low-fat milk or reconstituted low-fat
powdered milk. Unlimited sugarless tea and coffee with
milk from allowance, and slimmers' low-calorie drinks.

Breakfast

1 egg (size 4), boiled
1 slice slimmers' bread spread with 3g/⅛oz low-fat spread such
as Gold or Outline

Lunch
227g/8oz packet Findus shepherd's pie
75g/3oz green beans
1 orange

Evening meal
200g/7oz (raw weight) lean ham steak, grilled and topped with
1 canned pineapple ring and 25g/1oz grated Edam cheese and
heated under grill until cheese is melted
2 grilled tomatoes
50g/2oz sweetcorn

—————— Menu No. 7 ——————

Drinks allowance:
275ml/½ pint silver-top milk *or* 550ml/1 pint skimmed
or separated milk, plus unlimited tea and coffee without
sugar. Also as much of slimmers' low-calorie drinks and
water as you like.

Breakfast
2 Weetabix
125ml/4 fl. oz milk (extra to allowance)
5ml/1 level teaspoon sugar

Lunch
113g/4oz carton cottage cheese with chives
2 sticks celery
2 crispbreads spread with 7g/¼oz butter or 15g/½oz low-fat
spread
1 orange

Evening meal
142g/5oz pack Birds Eye braised kidneys in gravy
75g/3oz frozen mixed vegetables, boiled
1 small banana

Menu No. 8

Drinks allowance:
275ml/½ pint silver-top milk *or* 550ml/1 pint skimmed
or separated milk, plus unlimited tea and coffee without
sugar. Also as much of slimmers' low-calorie drinks and
water as you like.

Breakfast
25g/1oz slice wholemeal bread, toasted and spread with
7g/¼oz butter
5ml/1 teaspoon marmalade

Lunch
2 eggs (size 5), hard-boiled
15ml/1 tablespoon low-calorie salad dressing mixed salad of
lettuce, tomato, watercress and cucumber
1 pear or peach

Evening meal
1 Birds Eye Quarterpounder beefburger, well grilled
142g/5oz Heinz spaghetti with cheese and tomato sauce
1 Ross Devonshire strawberry trifle

Menu No. 9

Drinks allowance:
275ml/½ pint silver-top milk and unlimited sugarless tea
and coffee, and slimmers' low-calorie drinks.

Breakfast
1 egg (size 4), poached
1 slice slimmers' bread, toasted and spread lightly with low-fat
spread

Lunch
113g/4oz pack Ross Roast Beef with Gravy
½ x 64g/2.26oz packet Cadbury Smash reconstituted
according to directions
75g/3oz boiled cabbage, greens or Brussels sprouts
150g/5oz slice of canteloupe or yellow melon

Evening meal
283g/10oz can Crosse and Blackwell chicken curry and rice
113g/4oz Mr Kipling apple and blackcurrant pie

Menu No. 10

Drinks allowance:
275ml/½ pint silver-top milk *or* 550ml/1 pint skimmed
or separated milk, plus unlimited tea and coffee without
sugar. Also as much slimmers' low-calorie drinks and
water as you like.

Breakfast
25g/1oz 30% bran flakes
75ml/3 fl. oz milk (extra to allowance)
5ml/1 level teaspoon sugar

Lunch
1 crusty roll with 7g/¼oz butter or 15g/½oz low-fat spread
50g/2oz lean ham with mustard and cress
1 apple

Evening meal
1 Findus Calorie Counter chilli con carne with mixed vegetables
1 orange

— Menu No. 11 —

Drinks allowance:
275ml/½ pint low-fat separated or skimmed milk and as
much sugarless tea and coffee and as many low-calorie
drinks as you wish.

Breakfast

170g/6oz pack Findus Scottish smoked haddock
3 tablespoons canned tomatoes
25g/1oz slice wholemeal bread (no butter)

Lunch

283g/10oz can Heinz low-calorie mushroom soup
255g/9oz Findus Calorie Counter chicken supreme with mixed
vegetables

Evening meal

2 Findus steak and kidney pancakes, shallow fried
125g/4oz boiled green beans
75g/3oz canned tomatoes
125g/4oz canned or frozen carrots

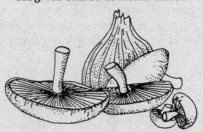

When recommended use one of the low-fat
milks instead of silver-top milk. This saves
calories.

Menu No. 12

Drinks allowance:
275ml/½ pint silver-top milk and as much sugarless tea
and coffee and low-calorie drinks as you wish.

Breakfast
½ grapefruit
1 egg (size 4), boiled
25g/1oz slice of bread, toasted, spread with 7g/¼oz butter

Lunch
2 frozen fish cakes, grilled without fat
1 grilled tomato
142g/5oz can of baked beans

Evening meal
227g/8oz pack Birds Eye Chinese Dragon sweet and sour
chicken
½ packet Birds Eye savoury vegetable rice

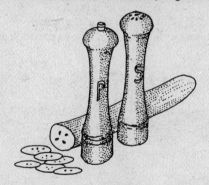

*Grill fish cakes and fish fingers without added
fat. They taste just as good.*

Menu No. 13

Drinks allowance:

275ml/½ pint silver-top milk for drinks. Unlimited sugarless tea and coffee, and slimmers' low-calorie drinks.

Breakfast

125g/4oz canned grapefruit segments in natural juice
1 Ryvita crispbread, spread with 3g/⅛oz butter

Lunch

2 frozen beefburgers, well-grilled
1 grilled tomato
75g/3oz boiled peas
10ml/1 dessertspoon brown sauce
1 orange

Evening meal

170g/6oz packet Birds Eye cod in parsley sauce
125g/4oz boiled potatoes
75g/3oz boiled Brussels sprouts
150g/5fl. oz carton Eden Vale fruit-flavoured yogurt

────── *Menu No. 14* ──────

Drinks allowance:
Unlimited sugarless tea and coffee and slimmers' low-calorie drinks.

Breakfast
25g/1oz cornflakes
150ml/¼ pint low-fat milk
1 rounded/5ml teaspoon sugar

Lunch
1 large thin 40g/1½oz slice bread toasted and lightly spread with 7g/¼oz low-fat spread, topped with 142g/5oz can baked beans
141g/5oz carton St Ivel or Farmer's Wife low-fat natural yogurt

Evening meal
1 individual Birds Eye chicken pie
75g/3oz boiled potatoes
75g/3oz boiled cabbage

Low-fat natural yogurt can be sweetened with low-calorie liquid sweetener if you can't face it unsweetened.

Breakfast Misser's Menus

Is it true that you must eat breakfast, when you are dieting?

In the view of Slimming magazine's experts it is not true; it is an outdated piece of advice which far too many dieticians have been handing out for far too long.

There is only one good reason for eating breakfast — and that is because you happen to feel hungry at breakfast time. If you don't happen to feel hungry at this time of day, there is no point at all in forcing down calories, and using up food which you might be yearning for later in the day.

Forcing down an unwanted breakfast does not, as many outdated slimming advisors seem to imagine, protect you from eating temptations throughout the morning. Eating temptations usually arise because of the sight, or scent of certain foods, or hundreds of other psychological appetite-triggering cues, and have very little to do with the state of your stomach.

As many people who have been skipping breakfast for years can confirm, the normal healthy adult will take no harm from missing breakfast.

The advantage of missing breakfast, for those who don't feel the need for it, is that it allows you to save those calories for the time of day when you often experience very strong desires to eat. Late evening, for instance, is a very high-temptation time for many slimmers.

In these menus we skip those breakfast calories and save them for an extra snack which can be eaten at the time of day when you are most tempted to eat.

——— Menu No. 1 ———

Drinks allowance:

Unlimited sugarless tea and coffee with milk from allowance, slimmers' low-calorie drinks and water.
275ml/½ pint low-fat skimmed milk or reconstituted low-fat powdered milk for drinks and cooking.

Fat allowance:

15g/½oz butter or margarine or 25g/1oz low-fat spread for spreading and cooking.

Lunch

75ml/3fl. oz natural orange juice
2 lamb's kidneys, grilled
1 grilled tomato
1 large thin slice white bread, lightly buttered
1 carton mustard and cress

Dinner
*Turkey parcel
125g/4oz boiled green beans
1 apple

Anytime snacks
156g/5½oz can condensed oxtail soup
125g/4oz black grapes

*Turkey parcel

Lightly grease a sheet of foil large enough to wrap a
175g/6oz turkey breast. Place 50g/2oz sweetcorn and
50g/2oz chopped green pepper on foil; season with salt
and pepper. Place turkey breast on top; season again.
Baste with 30ml/2 tablespoons orange juice, then seal foil
loosely around turkey. Bake at 400° F, 200° C, gas Mark
6 for 45 minutes. Remove turkey and vegetables from foil
and spoon cooking juices over the top.

————————*Menu No. 2*————————

Drinks allowance:
275ml/½ pint skimmed or separated milk. Unlimited
sugarless tea and coffee, slimmers' low-calorie drinks and
water.

Roast meal
75g/3oz portion roast chicken
thin gravy made from ¼ chicken stock cube, 60ml/4
tablespoons boiling water and thickened with 2.5ml/½ level
teaspoon cornflour
125g/4oz roast potatoes
75g/3oz Brussels sprouts, boiled
150g/5oz canned fruit salad

High tea

Egg mayonnaise salad: cut 1 hard-boiled (size 4) egg in half.
Place on a mixed salad of lettuce, cucumber, 4 spring onions, ½
tomato and a few rings of red pepper. Top the egg halves with
30ml/2 tablespoons low-calorie salad dressing such as
Waistline, then sprinkle with paprika
1 cream-filled meringue

Anytime snack
2 Nice biscuits

--------- # Menu No. 3 ---------

Drinks allowance:
275ml/½ pint silver-top milk. Unlimited sugarless tea
and coffee, slimmers' low-calorie drinks and water.

Light meal
113g/4oz carton Eden Vale cottage cheese topped with a
canned peach half
salad made from lettuce, watercress, 25g/1oz sliced cucumber,
1 sliced tomato and 4 spring onions
2 crispbreads spread with 15g/½oz low-fat spread

Main meal
227g/8oz Birds Eye tomato and cheese pizza
1 Findus Calorie-Counter mousse
125ml/4fl. oz glass dry red wine

Anytime snack
1 sachet Batchelor's beef and tomato Cup-a-Soup

Menu No. 4

Drinks allowance:
275ml/½ pint silver-top milk. Unlimited sugarless tea and coffee, water and slimmers' low-calorie drinks.

Light meal
1 average-size Scotch egg
salad made from lettuce, watercress, 2 sliced raw mushrooms, 1 grated carrot and 1 sliced tomato, dressed with fresh lemon juice

Main meal
1 packet Birds Eye crispy cod and chips, deep-fried as directed
75g/3oz boiled peas
1 apple or pear

Anytime snack
141g/5oz carton low-fat natural yogurt
1 orange

Menu No. 5

Drinks allowance:
275ml/½ pint skimmed or separated milk or reconstituted low-fat powdered milk.
Unlimited low-calorie drinks and sugarless tea and coffee.

Fat allowance:
15g/½oz butter or margarine or 25g/1oz low-fat spread for spreading and cooking.

Lunch
*Chicken liver, tomato and yogurt bake
125g/4oz boiled cabbage

Dinner
**Baked mackerel and mixed vegetables
25g/1oz slice wholemeal bread, lightly buttered
50g/2oz watercress
1 orange

Anytime snacks
142g/5oz can Heinz baked beans
25g/1oz slice wholemeal bread, lightly buttered

*Chicken liver, tomato and yogurt bake

Slice 1 tomato and place in bottom of a lightly greased ovenproof dish. Pour boiling water over 50g/2oz chicken livers, drain, then lay them on top of tomato. Season with salt and pepper. Season a 141g/5oz carton of low-fat natural yogurt with salt and pepper and blend in 15ml/1 tablespoon Worcestershire sauce. Pour yogurt over livers and tomato. Bake uncovered at 400° F, 200° C, gas Mark 6 for 25 minutes. Chop and lightly boil 125g/4oz cabbage and serve chicken liver, tomato and yogurt bake on top.

**Baked mackerel and mixed vegetables

Clean a 225g/8oz mackerel and season inside with salt and pepper, squeeze of lemon juice and a little chopped fresh parsley. Fold into shape and place on a lightly greased piece of foil. Place 50g/2oz mixed vegetables alongside the mackerel and seal foil into a parcel. Bake at 350° F, 180° C, gas Mark 4 for 30 minutes.

— *Menu No. 6*—

Drinks allowance:

275ml/½ pint silver-top milk for use in tea and coffee without sugar. Also as much low-calorie drinks and water as you like.

Light meal

1 sausage and 2 rashers streaky bacon, well-grilled
15ml/1 tablespoon brown sauce
150g/5oz baked beans
1 orange

Main meal

75g/3oz corned beef
mixed salad of lettuce, tomato, cress and spring onions
15ml/1 tablespoon low-calorie salad dressing
1 apple or pear

Anytime snack

150ml/5fl. oz carton fruit yogurt

Menu No. 7

Drinks allowance:
275ml/½ pint silver-top milk for use in tea and coffee without sugar. Also as much low-calorie drinks and water as you like.

Light meal
25g/1oz slice white or wholemeal bread
2 sardines in tomato sauce topped with 25g/1oz grated Edam cheese

Main meal
75g/3oz lean roast pork
45ml/3 tablespoons fatless gravy
15ml/1 tablespoon apple sauce
75g/3oz boiled carrots
75g/3oz boiled cabbage
fresh fruit salad made from ½ orange, ½ apple and 1 small banana, cut up and mixed together

Anytime snack
1 can Heinz mushroom or chicken or oxtail low-calorie soup
25g/1oz slice white or wholemeal bread

Always make gravy with stock, stock cubes or a gravy powder mixed with cold water. Never use fat from roasting tin.

—————— *Menu* No. 8 ——————

Drinks allowance:

Unlimited sugarless lemon tea and black coffee and slimmers' low-calorie drinks and water.

Light meal

Sandwich made from 2 slices of slimmers' bread and 3 rashers well-grilled streaky bacon, plus 15ml/1 tablespoon tomato sauce
1 orange

Main meal

*Shepherd's pie
75g/3oz boiled peas

Anytime snack

1 Ross frozen crème caramel
1 rich tea biscuit

*Shepherd's pie

Fry 175g/6oz raw minced beef until brown and drain off the fat. Add ½ an Oxo cube dissolved in 65ml/⅛ pint water and simmer for 5 minutes. Season. Boil 175g/6oz of potatoes and mash with 7g/¼oz butter and 15ml/1 tablespoon milk. Spoon the meat into a small ovenproof dish and spread the mashed potato over the top. Sprinkle 25g/1oz grated Cheddar cheese over potato and garnish with 1 sliced tomato. Put under the grill until the top is nicely browned.

————*Menu No. 9*————

Drinks allowance:

As many low-calorie drinks – water, unsugared lemon tea, black coffee and special slimmers' drinks – as you wish.

275ml/½ pint low-fat separated milk or reconstituted low-fat powdered milk for use in drinks and cooking.

Fat allowance:

15g/½oz butter or margarine or 25g/1oz low-fat spread for cooking and spreading.

Lunch

*Fish salad
1 orange

Evening meal

**Yogurt-topped baked chicken
125g/4oz runner beans
1 apple

Anytime snacks

125g/4oz green grapes
2 slices slimmers' bread, lightly buttered

*Fish salad

Put 175g/6oz cod or coley fillet in a pan, season with salt and pepper plus a dash of lemon juice, and just cover with water. Poach gently for 15 minutes, then drain and cool.

Cut fish into bite-size pieces. Finely chop 125g/4oz raw cabbage; grate 50g/2oz carrots. Place fish, cabbage, carrots and 15g/½oz raisins in a small bowl. Mix together 15ml/1 tablespoon low-calorie salad dressing, half a carton of low-fat natural yogurt, seasoning and a squeeze of lemon juice, and fold into the salad. Garnish with chopped parsley.

**Yogurt-topped baked chicken

Brown a 200g/7oz chicken joint under a hot grill for 5 minutes, then place in an ovenproof dish. Chop 1 stick of celery and mix with 125g/4oz canned tomatoes, season to taste and add a pinch of dried basil or thyme. Pour over chicken. Cover and bake at 375°F, 190°C, gas Mark 5 for 30 minutes. Uncover, then spoon half a carton of low-fat natural yogurt over the top. Cook uncovered for a further 5 minutes. Serve hot.

———*Menu No. 10*———

Drinks allowance:
275ml/½ pint silver-top milk and as much sugarless tea and coffee as you wish; also low-calorie drinks.

Morning
150ml/¼ pint unsweetened orange juice

Light meal
175g/6oz fillet white fish, poached, steamed or grilled
125g/4oz frozen mixed vegetables, boiled

Main meal
227g/8oz frozen shepherd's pie
125g/4oz boiled runner beans
125g/4oz boiled carrots

Anytime snacks
1 Penguin biscuit
2 cream crackers
15g/½oz portion cheese spread

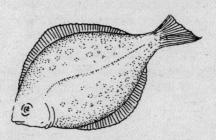

Always steam, poach, grill or bake white fish rather than fry it.

————Menu No. 11————

Drinks allowance:

275ml/½ pint low-fat skimmed milk or reconstituted low-fat powdered milk for drinks and cooking.
Unlimited sugarless tea and coffee with milk from allowance, slimmers' low-calorie drinks and water.

Fat allowance:

15g/½oz butter or margarine or 25g/1oz low-fat spread for spreading and cooking.

Lunch

1 crusty bread roll filled with 1 egg (size 4), hard-boiled, chopped and mixed with 50g/2oz prawns and 15ml/1 tablespoon Waistline.seafood sauce
1 orange

Dinner

125g/4oz lamb's liver, grilled
50g/2oz mushrooms, poached in stock
125g/4oz canned tomatoes
75g/3oz boiled cauliflower
175g/6oz cooking apple stewed with 125g/4oz blackberries and 5ml/1 teaspoon sugar

Anytime snacks

25g/1oz All-Bran cereal with milk from allowance
2 Ryvita crispbreads, lightly buttered
1 stick celery

——————Menu No. 12——————

Drinks allowance:
275ml/½ pint low-fat skimmed or separated milk. Unlimited sugarless tea and coffee, and slimmers' low-calorie drinks and water.

Light meal
*Tuna and apple salad
1 small banana

Main meal
**Spaghetti Bolognese
50g/2oz vanilla ice cream with ½ x 212g/7½oz can Mandarins in light syrup

Anytime snack
1 apple or orange with 141g/5oz carton low-fat natural yogurt
1 chocolate wholemeal *or* 1 plain digestive biscuit

*Tuna and apple salad

Drain all the oil off a 100g/3½oz can of tuna fish and roughly flake the fish. Core and dice 1 red-skinned eating apple and chop 1 stick of celery. Mix tuna, apple and celery with 15ml/1 tablespoon low-calorie salad dressing and 15ml/1 tablespoon vinegar. Season and pile onto a bed of shredded lettuce.

**Spaghetti Bolognese

Brown 125g/4oz raw minced beef in a non-stick pan, then drain off the fat and discard. Take 15ml/1 rounded tablespoon dry Minestrone soup powder and mix into mince. Stir in 150ml/¼ pint water, a dash of Worcestershire sauce and a little black pepper. Bring to the boil and simmer for 20 minutes. Boil 25g/1oz spaghetti until just tender, then drain. Pour the Bolognese sauce over the spaghetti and sprinkle with 5ml/1 teaspoon grated Parmesan cheese.

Remember to drain off and discard all the oil from canned fish. Use sardines in tomato sauce rather than sardines in oil to save calories.

—Working Girl's— Menus

These menus are designed to solve that 'what can I eat for lunch?' problem of the woman who goes out to work.

Restaurant meals, however carefully chosen, are never ideal for the slimmer who is trying to keep to a strict 1000 calories a day for speedy weight loss. Even the simplest dishes are subject to vast calorie variation. How can you tell how much fat the restaurant or canteen cook has used to fry an omelette, or whether that 'grilled' fish has been well-basted with fat?

Even restaurant salads can be far from safe. Oily dressings, often barely noticed, can turn salad concoctions into very fattening meals.

These menus allow the working girl to keep to her strict 1000 calories a day throughout the working week the only reliable way — by taking her calorie-counted lunch with her to work. Each menu includes an easily packed lunch.

—— *Menu No. 1* ——

Drinks allowance:
275ml/½ pint silver-top milk for use in tea and coffee. Unlimited sugarless tea and coffee, low-calorie drinks and water.

Breakfast
125g/4oz smoked haddock fillet, poached
1 egg (size 4), poached

Packed lunch
1 crusty bread roll with 7g/¼oz low-fat spread
113g/4oz carton cottage cheese with chives, or onion and peppers
watercress
1 orange

Evening meal
1 serving of Vesta paella
1 slice (175g/6oz) yellow or honeydew melon

When serving a slice of melon, sprinkle it with a little ground ginger rather than sugar.

— Menu No. 2 —

Drinks allowance:

275ml/½ pint silver-top milk for use in tea and coffee. Unlimited sugarless tea and coffee, low-calorie drinks and water.

Breakfast

175g/6oz prunes, stewed without sugar

Packed lunch

2 chipolata sausages, well-grilled
1 tomato
½ x 227g/8oz carton Matteson's coleslaw in vinaigrette
1 Ryvita crispbread scraped with low-fat spread

Evening meal

1 can Heinz low-calorie chicken soup
75g/3oz stewing steak cooked in Oxo stock with 50g/2oz onion, 75g/3oz carrot, 75g/3oz turnip, 125g/4oz boiled cabbage
1 carton Sainsbury's or Dessert Farm fruit yogurt

Menu No. 3

Drinks allowance:
275ml/½pint silver-top or 550ml/1 pint skimmed or
separated milk, plus unlimited sugarless tea and coffee,
water and low-calorie drinks.

Breakfast
½ grapefruit
25g/1oz 30% Bran Flakes
5ml/1 teaspoon sugar
75ml/3 fl. oz milk (additional to allowance)

Packed lunch
Tuna sandwich made from 2 slices slimmers' bread, 7g/¼oz
low-fat spread, 40g/1½oz drained, canned tuna, 5ml/1
teaspoon tomato chutney and watercress
1 apple

Evening meal
*Liver and mushroom casserole
150g/5oz boiled cauliflower
1 St Ivel fruit fool or Ross mousse

*Liver and mushroom casserole

Put 125g/4oz lamb's liver in a small casserole. Add
50g/2oz sliced mushrooms, ½ stick celery, sliced, 1
tomato, skinned and chopped and a pinch of mixed
herbs. Dissolve ½ beef stock cube in 75ml/3 fl. oz water.
Blend 5ml/1 level teaspoon cornflour with a little water
and add to stock. Bring to the boil, stirring continuously.
Pour over the liver, cover and bake at 350°F, 180°C, gas
Mark 4 for 45 minutes. serve with boiled cauliflower.

—— *Menu No. 4* ——

Drinks allowance:
275ml/½ pint low-fat skimmed milk or reconstituted low-fat powdered milk for drinks. As much sugarless tea and coffee and slimmers' low-calorie drinks as you wish.

Breakfast
1 egg (size 4), boiled
2 slices slimmers' bread, toasted
7g/¼oz low-fat spread

Lunch
A Wimpy burger (no extras)
1 orange

Evening meal
165g/5½oz pork chop, well-grilled
2 grilled tomatoes
45ml/3 tablespoons thin gravy without fat
100g/4oz mashed potato without fat or milk
125g/4oz boiled green beans

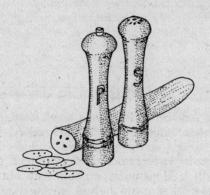

Menu No. 5

Drinks allowance:

275ml/½ pint silver-top *or* 550ml/1 pint skimmed or separated milk, plus unlimited sugarless tea and coffee. Also as much water and as many low-calorie drinks as you wish.

Breakfast

125ml/4 fl. oz orange juice
1 slice slimmers' bread, toasted, with scrape of low-fat spread
5ml/1 teaspoon marmalade

Packed lunch

75g/3oz lean cooked ham
mixed salad of lettuce, cress, spring onions, tomato, cucumber and celery (all packed in a plastic box)
1 Ryvita with a scrape of low-fat spread
1 Eden Vale chocolate, chocolate and mint or chocolate and orange dessert

Evening meal

75g/3oz roast chicken
30ml/2 tablespoons fatless gravy
75g/3oz boiled carrots
75g/3oz boiled cauliflower
1 Ross crème caramel

Choose lean, boiled ham rather than fatty ham or roasted ham. Remove any visible fat.

Menu No. 6

Drinks allowance:
275ml/½ pint low-fat skimmed milk. Unlimited sugar-less tea and coffee, water and low-calorie drinks.

Breakfast
1 egg (size 4), poached
1 slice slimmers' bread, toasted and scraped with low-fat spread

Packed lunch
4 Ryvitas spread with 15g/½oz low-fat spread, 50g/2oz grated
Edam cheese and 2 tomatoes
1 orange

Evening meal
3 frozen fish fingers, grilled without fat
142g/5oz can baked beans
1 Birds Eye orange and lemon or chocolate mousse

—————— *Menu No. 7*——————

Drinks allowance:

275ml/½ pint silver-top milk for tea and coffee. Unlimited sugarless tea and coffee, low-calorie drinks and water.

Breakfast

20g/¾oz Rice Krispies
75ml/3 fl. oz silver-top milk (additional to drink allowance)
1 rounded 5ml/teaspoon sugar

Packed lunch

2 × 25g/1oz slices of wholemeal bread spread with 15g/½oz low-fat spread and filled with 40g/1½oz liver sausage and watercress or mustard and cress

Evening meal

142g/5oz pack Birds Eye braised kidneys in gravy
150g/5oz boiled potatoes
75g/3oz Brussels sprouts
1 orange

—————— *Menu No. 8* ——————

Drinks allowance:

275ml/½ pint silver-top milk. As much sugarless tea and coffee and as many low-calorie drinks as you wish.

Breakfast

2 rashers streaky bacon, well-grilled
1 grilled tomato
1 slice slimmers' bread, unbuttered

Packed lunch

4 slices slimmers' bread with 15g/½oz low-fat spread and a
filling of 50g/2oz canned salmon, drained, and 50g/2oz sliced
cucumber
1 apple or orange

Evening meal

250g/9oz raw weight chicken joint, foil-baked
60ml/4 tablespoons gravy made without fat
125g/4oz boiled carrots
125g/4oz boiled Brussels sprouts
1 Wall's strawberry mousse

———— *Menu No. 9* ————

Drinks allowance:

275ml/½ pint silver-top milk. As much sugarless tea and
coffee and as many low-calorie drinks as you wish.

Breakfast

125ml/4 fl. oz orange juice
1 egg (size 4), poached on 1 slice slimmers' bread, toasted and
spread with 3g/⅛oz butter

Packed lunch

Batchelor's chicken noodle Cup-a-Soup
2 crispbreads lightly spread with 7g/¼oz butter
40g/1½oz Edam cheese
1 tomato

Evening meal

165g/5½oz (raw weight) lean lamb chump chop, well-grilled
50g/2oz boiled peas
75g/3oz boiled carrots
60ml/4 tablespoons gravy made without fat
1 orange or apple

Menu No. 10

Drinks allowance:
275ml/½ pint low-fat skimmed milk for use in sugarless tea and coffee. Unlimited slimmers' low-calorie drinks and water.

Breakfast
25g/1oz cornflakes
1 rounded/5ml teaspoon sugar
75ml/3 fl. oz skimmed milk (additional to allowance)

Packed lunch
1 double decker sandwich using 3 slices slimmers' bread,
7g/¼oz low-fat spread, 50g/2oz corned beef,
1.25ml/¼ teaspoon horseradish sauce, and 15g/½oz portion
cheese spread with 5ml/1 teaspoon sweet pickle
2 sticks celery
2 finger Kit-Kat

Evening meal
1 Findus Calorie Counter Beef Chasseur or
Chilli con carne
1 orange

—Dine-with-the— Family Menus

For many dieters, the evening or main meal is a social family occasion. Housewives, who often lunch alone, don't want to have to dine alone as well. Neither do they want to have to cook a special meal for themselves — at a time when they are cooking the main meal of the day for the family.

These 1000-calorie menus are specially planned to allow for a family meal, which is usually in the evening during the week and can be either at lunch time or in the evening at the weekend according to the family's timetable. The family meals which have been devised are the kind of popular everyday dishes which appear on most family menus. Nothing 'sacrificial' about them! You save calories by being strict and careful on quantity — rather than cooking special made-for-slimmers dishes.

We have given precise instructions for your own portion of the family meal. Using the same basic dishes you can increase the quantity cooked to feed the rest of the family too. And, of course, those who have no weight problems might have additional potatoes, puddings, sauces, etc. On these dieting menus you can all eat the same dinner, and dieters only have to eat less of it than other family members.

——————*Menu No. 1*——————

Drinks allowance:
275ml/½ pint low-fat skimmed milk or reconstituted low-fat powdered milk, plus unlimited sugarless tea and coffee. Also unlimited slimmers' low-calorie drinks and water.

Fat allowance:
15g/½oz butter or margarine or 25g/1oz low-fat spread for spreading and cooking.

Breakfast
½ grapefruit
1 egg (size 5), boiled or poached
25g/1oz slice wholemeal bread, toasted if you wish

Lunch
Open sandwich using 25g/1oz slice wholemeal bread, lightly buttered and topped with 1 drained canned pineapple ring and 113g/4oz carton cottage cheese
salad made from a few sprigs watercress, few lettuce leaves and 25g/1oz cucumber (no dressing)

Dinner
½ grapefruit
125g/4oz lean steak, grilled
1 grilled tomato
125g/4oz boiled potatoes
125g/4oz cooked spinach
125g/4oz fresh or frozen strawberries mixed with 1 chopped
pineapple ring

*If you find grapefruit too tart to eat as they
are, cut out flesh and mix with a little liquid
sweetener.*

Menu No. 2

Drinks allowance:

Unlimited sugarless tea and coffee with milk from
allowance and slimmers' low-calorie drinks.
275ml/½ pint low-fat skimmed milk or reconstituted
low-fat powdered milk for drinks and cereal.

Fat allowance:

15g/½oz butter or margarine or 25g/1oz low-fat spread
for spreading and cooking.

Breakfast

25g/1oz All-Bran with milk from allowance
1 egg (size 5), boiled or poached
50g/2oz crusty bread roll, lightly buttered

Lunch

50g/2oz prawns with 1 stick celery, chopped and mixed with
15ml/1 tablespoon low-calorie salad dressing
50g/2oz watercress
2 Ryvita crispbreads, lightly buttered
1 orange

Dinner

*Braised liver
75g/3oz cauliflower, boiled
**Baked apple with blackberry sauce

*Braised liver (1 serving)

If you wish to make this dish for the whole family, just multiply the quantities by the number of persons. Heat 125g/4oz canned tomatoes with 25g/1oz chopped onion, 50g/2oz sliced mushrooms, pinch mixed herbs, salt and pepper, and a dash of Worcestershire Sauce in a covered pan for 10 minutes. Pour boiling water over 125g/4oz lamb's liver, then drain. Lay liver in bottom of a lightly greased casserole dish. Season and pour the tomato mixture and herbs over the liver and bake at 350°F, 180°C Gas Mark 4 for 30 minutes. Alternatively this could be gently cooked on top of the stove.

**Baked apple with blackberry sauce (1 serving)

Wash and core a 175g/6oz cooking apple. Slit all round through skin only. Pack 25g/1oz blackberries into core hole of the apple, and place in a small ovenproof dish with a little water. Cover with foil and bake at 350°F, 180°C, gas Mark 4 for 30 minutes, or until apple is cooked but still whole. Cook 75g/3oz blackberries in a little water with 5ml/1 teaspoon sugar until soft. Sieve and add artificial sweetener to taste, if wished. Serve baked apple with hot blackberry sauce poured over.

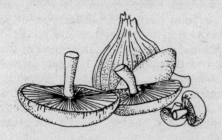

Menu No. 3

Drinks allowance:
185ml/⅓ pint silver-top milk *or* 275ml/½ pint low-fat milk (separated or reconstituted dried) plus unlimited water, sugarless tea and coffee, and slimmers' low-calorie drinks.

Breakfast
125ml/4 fl. oz unsweetened orange juice
4 tablespoons (15g/½oz) cornflakes or bran flakes
1 sliced banana (150g/5oz)
milk from allowance

Light meal
*Mushroom omelette with ratatouille
2 crispbreads
15g/½oz portion cheese spread

Main meal
275ml/½ pint Knorr minestrone soup
**Cottage pie
50g/2oz boiled peas
1 apple, orange or pear

*Mushroom omelette with ratatouille (1 serving)

Slice 2 tomatoes, 2 courgettes, 1 small green pepper, 1 stick of celery and 1 small onion. Place in a pan with 15ml/1 tablespoon water and salt to taste. Cover and simmer gently until the vegetables are tender. Poach 50g/2oz button mushrooms in a little water or stock for 5 minutes, and then drain. Whisk 2 eggs (size 4) and 30ml/2 tablespoons water together. Season. Melt 3g/⅛oz butter in a non-stick omelette pan and pour in the eggs. Cook gently until set. Fill the omelette with poached mushrooms and serve with the vegetables (ratatouille).

**Cottage pie (1 serving)

Fry 125g/4oz minced beef in a non-stick pan (without additional fat) until brown. Drain off any fat. Dissolve ½ beef stock cube in 150ml/¼ pint hot water. Add to the minced beef with 25g/1oz chopped onion and a pinch mixed herbs. Simmer for 30 minutes. Season to taste. Meanwhile, boil 175g/6oz parsnip. Drain and mash with 3g/⅛oz butter and a little milk from allowance. Put the cooked mince in a small ovenproof dish and top with mashed parsnip and 1 sliced tomato. Grill until top is golden. Serve with peas.

Menu No. 4

Drinks allowance:
275ml/½ pint low-fat separated or skimmed milk. Unlimited sugarless tea and coffee and slimmers' low-calorie drinks.

Breakfast
½ grapefruit
1 thin slice bread from a large loaf, toasted and lightly spread with low-fat spread
1 heaped teaspoon marmalade

Light meal
2 large beef or pork sausages, well-grilled
1 egg (size 5), poached
1 slice slimmers' bread without butter

Main meal
*Baked potato with chicken livers and mushrooms
125g/4oz boiled broccoli
1 apple

*Baked potato with chicken livers and mushrooms (1 serving)

Bake a 175g/6oz potato in the oven at 400°F, 200°C, or gas Mark 6 for ¾ hour or until soft. Meanwhile gently fry in 7g/¼oz butter or margarine in a non-stick pan 75g/3oz chopped chicken livers and 25g/1oz sliced mushrooms for 5 minutes. Season well and add a dash Worcestershire sauce. Cut the potato into halves, scoop out the inside and mix the potato with the liver and mushroom mixture. Pile back into the potato cases. Serve hot.

Menu No. 5

This menu is designed for the mother who cannot resist a tea-time snack with the children.

Drinks allowance:

275ml/½ pint silver-top milk. Unlimited sugarless tea and coffee with milk from allowance and slimmers' low-calorie drinks or water.

Breakfast

½ grapefruit topped with 15g/½oz mincemeat and grilled until hot

Light meal

128g/4½oz Heinz chicken and mushroom toast topper spread on 2 slices toasted slimmers' bread and grilled with 2 tomatoes
1 apple

Tea-time

1 tea cake (50g/2oz) toasted and spread with 7g/¼oz butter or 15g/½oz low-fat spread and 5ml/1 teaspoon jam

Main meal

Average pork chop (165g/5½oz raw), grilled till crisp
45ml/3 tablespoons thin gravy, made without fat
50g/2oz boiled spinach
75g/3oz boiled carrots
1 dessertspoon apple sauce

Menu No. 6

Drinks allowance:

275ml/½ pint low-fat skimmed milk or reconstituted low-fat powdered milk. Unlimited low-calorie drinks – water, sugarless lemon tea and black coffee, and special slimmers' drinks.

Fat allowance:

15g/½oz butter or margarine or 25g/1oz low-fat spread for spreading and cooking

Breakfast

142g/5oz Heinz baked beans on 25g/1oz slice wholemeal bread lightly buttered

Light meal

*Chicken livers on toast
1 sliced tomato
50g/2oz watercress

Main meal

225g/8oz grilled mackerel
50g/2oz frozen mixed vegetables, boiled
125g/4oz cabbage, boiled
1 orange, segmented and stirred into 1 small carton low-fat natural yogurt

*Chicken livers on toast (1 serving)

Heat 3g/⅛oz butter from allowance with 30ml/2 tablespoons water, in a small pan. Chop 50g/2oz chicken livers and add to pan with seasoning and lemon juice. Cover and cook gently for 10 minutes. Serve on 25g/1oz slice of wholemeal bread, toasted.

——————*Menu No. 7*——————

Drinks allowance:

150ml/¼ pint low-fat skimmed milk or reconstituted low-fat powdered milk. Unlimited sugarless tea and coffee with milk from allowance and slimmers' low-calorie drinks.

Breakfast

2 chipolata sausages, well grilled
125g/4oz canned tomatoes, heated and seasoned to taste
1 slice unbuttered slimmers' bread

Light meal

25g/1oz slice bread, toasted. Top with 2 sardines in tomato sauce and 20g/¾oz grated Cheddar cheese. Grill until cheese melts

Main meal

*Liver casserole
100g/4oz jacket baked potato
**Baked banana

*Liver casserole (1 serving)

Slice 125g/4oz lamb's liver and finely chop 25g/1oz onion. Peel and slice a small 125g/4oz cooking apple. Place the liver, onion and apple in a small ovenproof dish. Season with salt, pepper and a pinch of mixed herbs. Pour over 125ml/4 fl. oz beef stock. Cover and bake at 400°F, 200°C, gas Mark 6 for 45 minues.

**Baked banana (1 serving)

Peel a 175g/6oz banana and slice in half lengthwise. Place in a lightly greased ovenproof dish, pour over the juice of 1 orange. Cover and bake at the same temperature as the liver casserole for about 25 minutes. Sprinkle 5ml/1 teaspoon desiccated coconut over the baked banana and serve hot.

Menu No. 8

Drinks allowance:
As much sugarless tea and coffee without milk and as much low-calorie drinks and water as you like.

Breakfast
25g/1oz All-Bran
75ml/3 fl. oz skimmed or separated milk
5ml/1 level teaspoon sugar (optional)

Dinner
75g/3oz roast leg of lamb
10ml/1 dessertspoon mint sauce
100g/4oz roast potato
75g/3oz carrots or swede, boiled
75g/3oz cauliflower

High tea
Prawn salad, made from 50g/2oz prawns, 10ml/1 dessertspoon low-calorie salad dressing, 1 tomato, 25g/1oz cucumber, lettuce leaves, 4 spring onions and mustard and cress.
1 toasted teacake spread with 7g/¼oz butter or 15g/½oz low-fat spread

Roast potatoes — leave the potatoes whole or cut into large chunks so that they absorb less fat.

—————Menu No. 9—————

Drinks allowance:

Unlimited sugarless lemon tea, black coffee and low-calorie drinks.

Breakfast

1 egg (size 4), boiled
1 Ryvita with a scrape of low-fat spread

Dinner

75g/3oz lean roast beef (cut off all fat before weighing)
45ml/3 tablespoons thin gravy, made without fat
2 average-size chunks of roast potato (100g/4oz)
75g/3oz boiled Brussels sprouts
50g/2oz boiled carrots
25g/1oz Yorkshire pudding
125g/4oz portion fresh fruit salad made from apple, orange,
banana, mixed with a little low-calorie lemonade or ginger ale

Evening meal

Vegetable omelette: use 2 eggs (size 4), 30ml/2 tablespoons
water and seasoning. Cook in a non-stick pan with 7g/¼oz
butter. Fill omelette with 15g/½oz chopped green pepper, 1
sliced tomato and a few raw button mushrooms
1 apple

Menu No. 10

Drinks allowance:
275ml/½ pint low-fat skimmed milk or reconstituted low-fat powdered milk. Unlimited sugarless tea and coffee, slimmers' low-calorie drinks and water.

Breakfast
½ grapefruit

Dinner
75g/3oz roast chicken
45ml/3 tablespoons thin gravy, no fat
125g/4oz roast potato
125g/4oz boiled broccoli
75g/3oz boiled carrots
100g/4oz cooking apple stewed with 5ml/1 teaspoon sugar
1 portion (100ml) Weight Watchers ice cream

Evening meal
1 large thin slice bread (40g/1½oz) toasted with 40g/1½oz
grated Edam cheese grilled on top
2 grilled tomatoes

Any time
1 Jacob's chocolate wholemeal biscuit

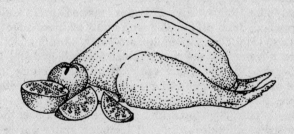

Menu No. 11

Drinks allowance:

As much sugarless tea and coffee without milk and as many drinks such as low-calorie squashes, PLJ, Slimlines and water as you like.

Breakfast

1 egg (size 4), scrambled with 30ml/2 tablespoons silver-top milk and served on 1 slice slimmers' bread, toasted

Light meal

2 frozen fish cakes, grilled without fat
100g/4oz canned tomatoes
141g/5oz carton low-fat natural yogurt served with 1 peeled and sliced orange

Main meal

*Potato moussaka
75g/3oz boiled cabbage

*Potato moussaka (1 serving)

Parboil a 125g/4oz peeled potato for 5 minutes, drain and slice thinly. Fry 175g/6oz minced beef until browned; drain off fat. Mix with 5ml/1 teaspoon onion flakes, 15ml/1 tablespoon tomato purée, 45ml/3 tablespoons water, salt and pepper, pinch oregano, and 5ml/1 teaspoon Worcestershire sauce. Place beef mixture in the base of a lightly greased ovenproof dish. Cover with sliced potato. Mix 141g/5oz carton St Ivel or St Michael low-fat natural yogurt with 1 egg (size 5). Pour over the potatoes. Sprinkle with 5ml/1 teaspoon grated Parmesan cheese. Place on middle shelf of a moderate oven, 350°F, 180°C, gas Mark 4 for 30 minutes.

Always pre-fry minced beef and drain off fat before adding other ingredients.

Menu No. 12

Drinks allowance:

As much sugarless black coffee and lemon tea as you like, also slimmers' low-calorie drinks and water.

Breakfast

25g/1oz slice white or wholemeal bread, toasted
150g/5oz baked beans
10ml/1 dessertspoon tomato sauce

Light meal

4 frozen cod fish fingers, grilled without fat
125g/4oz boiled runner beans
1 apple

Main meal

*Grilled corned beef savoury

*Grilled corned beef savoury (1 serving)

Fry a small chopped onion in 15g/½oz butter. Add 50g/2oz chopped corned beef, season with salt and pepper and add ½ an Oxo cube dissolved in ½ cup of water. Add 125g/4oz sliced boiled potato. Transfer to a shallow ovenproof dish and top with 40g/1½oz grated Cheddar cheese and 1 tomato, sliced. Place under hot grill until the cheese has melted.

Menu No. 13

Drinks allowance:

275ml/½ pint low-fat skimmed milk or 150ml/¼ pint silver-top milk, plus unlimited sugarless tea, coffee, water and low-calorie drinks.

Breakfast

2 rashers streaky bacon, well-grilled
1 egg (size 4), fried
1 slice slimmers' bread, unbuttered

Light meal

2 frozen beefburgers, well-grilled
142g/5oz can baked beans
1 orange

Main meal

225g/8oz chicken joint, grilled and served with a sauce made by heating ½ × 298g/10½oz can condensed vegetable soup with 30ml/2 tablespoons water and 5ml/1 level teaspoon concentrated curry sauce
75g/3oz boiled cauliflower
75g/3oz boiled green beans

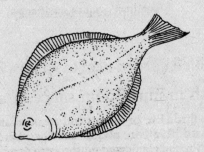

————————Menu No. 14————————

This menu is designed for the mother who cannot resist a mid-morning or tea-time snack with the children.

Drinks allowance:

275ml/½ pint silver-top *or* 550ml/1 pint skimmed or separated milk, plus unlimited sugarless tea, coffee, water and low-calorie drinks.

Breakfast

1 egg (size 4), boiled
1 crispbread with a scrape of low-fat spread

Mid-morning or tea-time

1 Jacob's Club biscuit

Light meal

113g/4oz carton cottage-cheese-and-pineapple
mixed salad of lettuce, tomato and chopped celery
2 crispbreads with 7g/¼oz low-fat spread

Main meal

*Fish in mushroom sauce
75g/3oz peas, boiled
100g/4oz courgettes, boiled
125g/4oz strawberries, fresh or frozen
30ml/2 tablespoons single cream

*Fish in mushroom sauce (1 serving)

Place a Birds Eye or Findus cod steak in an ovenproof dish with 25g/1oz peeled prawns. Spread half a 156/5½oz can condensed mushroom soup over fish and cook for 30 minutes at 400°F, 200°C, gas Mark 6. Serve with peas and courgettes.

—Slim-and-Sin—
Menus

Yes, 'a little of what you fancy' in the way of alcohol, chocolate, crisps, can do you good when you are dieting!

In the menus in this chapter we have included a daily indulgence in the form of the kind of drink or snack which many slimmers struggle to avoid because they consider it to be 'sinful'. In fact, struggling too hard to avoid all those sweet and starchy extras can be a dangerous policy for many slimmers. By eliminating all indulgent foods from their menus they often overtax their determination, succumb to cravings — then end up abandoning their diets completely because they have broken the rules.

No food need be a 'sinful' or fattening food. All foods can be included, in the right quantity, in a dieting menu. One calorie of chocolate, or chips, or gin, is no more *fattening than one calorie of lettuce or cottage cheese. As far as your weight loss is concerned, it is only the number of calories consumed each day which count — not the type of calories!*

However, obviously it wouldn't be wise to try to diet on 1000-calories worth of chocolate each day. This kind of diet would lack necessary nutrients, and provide you with such a small quantity of food that you would be hungry.

If you are tempted by certain snack foods and drinks the sensible thing is to include them in modest controlled quantities as part of the daily 1000 calories, as we have in these menus.

Many slimmers tell us that, when they are allowed a ration of their favourite snack-foods and drinks, they cease to crave these foods.

Try these menus if your diets normally collapse because of real yearnings for sweet and starchy foods or a comforting 'tipple'.

Some readers may find it helpful to turn to these menus on certain appropriate days, interspersing them between menus from other sections of this book.

—————— *Menu No. 1* ——————

Drinks allowance:

Unlimited sugarless lemon tea, black coffee, Bovril, Marmite and slimmers' low-calorie drinks, plus the 'sin' (see below).

Breakfast

1 whole grapefruit, segmented and sprinkled with 1 rounded
teaspoon of sugar
2 rashers streaky bacon, well grilled
1 grilled tomato

Lunch

283g/10oz can Heinz low-calorie Scotch broth or vegetable
and beef soup
25g/1oz slice of bread, toasted, topped with 40g/1½oz grated
Edam cheese and grilled
1 tomato

Evening meal

1 average lean lamb chump chop (165g/5½oz raw),
well grilled
15ml/1 tablespoon mint sauce
30ml/2 tablespoons thin gravy, made without fat
150g/5oz boiled potatoes
75g/3oz boiled carrots

Sin

550ml/1 pint lager, bitter beer or dry cider *or* 3 pub measures
whisky or gin (but only low-calorie mixers)

————— *Menu No. 2* —————

Drinks allowance:

Unlimited sugarless tea, black coffee, Bovril, Marmite
and slimmers' low-calorie drinks. Don't forget, water
adds nothing.

Breakfast

1 whole kipper (175g/6oz raw), grilled with 7g/¼oz butter
and served with a 25g/1oz slice brown bread spread with
3g/⅛oz butter

Lunch
75g/3oz cold roast chicken
salad made from lettuce, watercress, 4 spring onions, 25g/1oz
sliced cucumber and 1 sliced tomato

Evening meal
Scrambled eggs: heat 50ml/2 fl. oz silver top milk with 7g/¼oz
butter in a non-stick pan. Stir in 2 eggs (size 4) and seasoning
to taste. Serve on 25g/1oz slice of bread, toasted

Sin
2 fingers Kit-Kat

——————*Menu No. 3*——————

Drinks allowance:
275ml/½ pint silver-top milk. Unlimited sugarless tea,
coffee and slimmers' low-calorie drinks and water.

Breakfast
2 rashers back bacon, well-grilled
2 grilled tomatoes

Lunch
170g/6oz pack Birds Eye minced beef in gravy
75g/3oz carrots, boiled
50g/2oz peas

Evening meal
Onion omelette: fry 50g/2oz chopped onion in a non-stick pan
with 10g/⅓oz butter until onion is softened, then add 2
well-beaten eggs (size 4) with 30ml/2 tablespoons water. Cook
until just set
1 apple

Sin
1 Rowntree Mackintosh Walnut Whip, vanilla or coffee

Menu No. 4

Drinks allowance:
275ml/½ pint low-fat skimmed milk to use in sugarless tea and coffee. As much low-calorie drinks, PLJ, Bovril, Marmite and water as you like.

Breakfast

1 egg (size 4), poached
1 slice slimmers' bread, unbuttered

Lunch

3 fish fingers, grilled without fat
50g/2oz peas
15ml/1 tablespoon tomato sauce

Evening Meal

Spaghetti Bolognese: 40g/1½oz spaghetti, boiled and drained, topped with ½ can Campbell's Bolognese sauce
1 orange

Sin

1 jam doughnut

—————Menu No. 5—————

Drinks allowance:

275ml/½ pint low-fat skimmed or separated milk. Unlimited sugarless tea and coffee (with milk from allowance); also low-calorie drinks and water.

Breakfast

25g/1oz 30% bran flakes
150ml/¼ pint skimmed milk, additional to allowance

Lunch

Cheese and tomato sandwich made from 2 slices slimmers' bread, 25g/1oz Edam cheese, and 1 tomato, sliced
150g/5 fl. oz carton Ski or St Michael fruit-flavoured yogurt

Evening meal

150g/6oz white fish, grilled using 7g/¼oz butter or margarine
75g/3oz green beans
50g/2oz sweetcorn
1 orange, apple or pear

Sin

2 glasses (115ml/4 fl. oz) dry white wine

Hard cheese such as Edam will go further in salads and sandwiches if you grate it.

——Menu No. 6——

Drinks allowance:

275ml/½ pint low-fat skimmed milk to use in sugarless tea and coffee. As many low-calorie drinks and as much PLJ, Bovril, Marmite and water as you like.

Breakfast

150ml/¼ pint unsweetened orange juice
1 egg (size 4), boiled
2 crispbreads, scraped with low-fat spread

Lunch (packed)

4 crispbreads or 3 slices slimmers' bread scraped with low-fat spread plus *one* of the following fillings:
25g/1oz Cheddar cheese *or* 40g/1½oz Edam cheese *or* 125g/4oz cottage cheese with 1 tomato, cucumber slices and sprigs of watercress
1 apple, orange or pear

Evening meal

75g/3oz ham steak, grilled and topped with 1 canned pineapple ring
1 grilled tomato
50g/2oz sweetcorn

Sin

Wall's Golden Vanilla Choc Ice or Lyons Maid Dark Satin Choc Ice

—Menu No. 7—

Drinks allowance:
275ml/½ pint low-fat skimmed milk and unlimited sugarless tea and coffee (with milk from allowance); also low-calorie drinks, Bovril, Marmite and water.

Breakfast
½ grapefruit (no sugar)
2 slices slimmers' bread *or* 25g/1oz slice brown or white bread, toasted
7g/¼oz low-fat spread
5ml/1 teaspoon jam or marmalade

Lunch
225g/8oz chicken joint, foil-baked or roasted
mixed salad without dressing
1 apple, orange or pear

Evening meal
Kidneys in scrambled egg: grill 2 lamb's kidneys, chop them and add to scrambled egg mixture made with 2 eggs (size 4) and 30ml/2 tablespoons milk from drinks' allowance, plus seasoning, cooked in 7g/¼oz butter
1 grilled tomato
50g/2oz mushrooms, poached in a little stock

Sin
1 small packet of crisps (any flavour) *or* 1 small packet Hula Hoops

Instead of frying mushrooms, poach them in stock. They will taste better this way and save a great many calories.

Menu No. 8

Drinks allowance:

275ml/½ pint low-fat skimmed milk and unlimited sugarless tea and coffee (with milk from allowance); also low-calorie drinks, Bovril, Marmite and water.

Breakfast

125g/4oz prunes, stewed without sugar
1 egg (size 6), boiled
1 crispbread, scraped with low-fat spread

Lunch

2 frozen fish cakes, grilled without fat
150g/5oz baked beans

Evening meal

75g/3oz lean roast beef
45ml/3 tablespoons unthickened, fatless gravy
125g/4oz cabbage, greens or sprouts, boiled
75g/3oz carrots, boiled

Sin

1 Eden Vale fruit fool or St Ivel cream dessert
or St Michael strawberry fresh cream soufflé

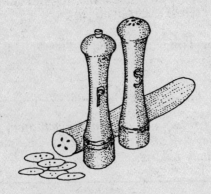

———— *Menu No. 9*————

Drinks allowance:

275ml/½ pint low-fat skimmed milk and unlimited sugarless tea and coffee (with milk from allowance); also low-calorie drinks, Bovril, Marmite and water.

Breakfast

25g/1oz black pudding, well-grilled
1 rasher back bacon, well-grilled
1 grilled tomato
1 slice slimmers' bread, unbuttered

Lunch

227g/8oz pack Ross shepherd's pie
75g/3oz runner beans

Evening meal

Smoked haddock kedgeree: mix 25g/1oz rice, boiled and drained with 175g/6oz smoked haddock fillet, cooked and flaked, and 7g/¼oz low-fat spread. Serve topped with 1 egg (size 4), hard-boiled and sliced and 1 sliced tomato
1 apple, orange or pear

Sin

2 slices bread (25g/1oz each) spread with 10g/⅓oz low-fat spread and 15g/½oz jam

————*Menu No. 10*————

Drinks allowance:
275ml/½ pint silver-top milk and as much sugarless tea and coffee and as many low-calorie drinks as you wish.

Breakfast
1 egg (size 4), boiled
1 crispbread, scraped with 3g/⅛oz butter

Lunch
170g/6oz pack Findus cod in parsley sauce
75g/3oz green beans
1 grilled tomato

Evening meal
1 large sausage, well-grilled
1 rasher streaky bacon, well-grilled
1 egg (size 6) fried
125g/4oz mushrooms, poached in stock
1 grilled tomato
slice slimmers' bread (no butter)

Sins
1 Lyon's Junior Chocolate Roll
1 small packet of Hula Hoops

Sociable Slimming Menus

These are the 1000-calorie menus to which to turn on special occasions when you are either dining out, or entertaining guests at home.

In choosing a restaurant meal it is impossible to be absolutely sure of the number of calories you are consuming. But restaurant meals on our menus at least minimize the guesswork, and could be included from time to time (as opposed to 'frequently') during your dieting campaign.

When entertaining at home it is possible to keep accurately to your diet with delicious dishes which don't happen to be costly in calories.

—————*Menu No. 1*—————

This menu allows for a restaurant meal. We do not intend you to ask the waiter to weigh your portions before serving you; however, if you weigh your food portions at home you will be able to estimate the weight of your restaurant portions. Do remember to ask for your salad *without dressing*.

Drinks allowance:

Unlimited sugarless lemon tea, black coffee, water or slimmers' low-calorie drinks. No milk allowed. We have allowed a glass of wine with your restaurant meal.

Breakfast

½ grapefruit
1 egg (size 4), boiled
1 Ryvita spread with 3g/⅛oz low-fat spread

Light meal

170g/6oz pack Findus cod in parsley sauce
50g/2oz carrots, boiled
125g/4oz courgettes, boiled

Restaurant meal

125ml/4 fl. oz tomato juice
large lean lamb chump chop, well-grilled *or* 2 small lamb cutlets, well-grilled
mixed salad (without dressing)
75g/3oz portion average-thickness chips *or* 200g/7oz jacket baked potato with 3g/⅛oz butter
100g/3½oz portion Lyons Rum 'n' Raisin or coffee, vanilla or chocolate ice cream
1 glass dry red wine

—————*Menu No. 2*—————

This menu allows for a meal eaten out. We try to minimize guesswork, but we don't expect you to have the food weighed!

Drinks allowance:
Unlimited tea or coffee (without sugar) or low-calorie drinks. No milk allowed.

Breakfast
½ grapefruit (no sugar)

Light meal
125g/4oz white fish, grilled
1 tomato
125g/4oz runner beans

Restaurant meal
1 medium or dry sherry
slice melon without sugar
average-size fillet steak, grilled
medium baked potato with 3g/⅛oz butter
serving of broccoli
1 glass dry wine
low-calorie dessert like a water ice or sorbet

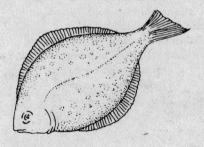

Menu No. 3

This is a menu with two rather special meals.

Drinks allowance:
Unlimited low-calorie drinks, e.g. water, sugarless black coffee and lemon tea, Slimline drinks, low-calorie squashes and PLJ.
1 glass dry white wine *or* dry red wine allowed with either lunch or evening meal.

Breakfast
1 egg (size 4), poached
1 slice unbuttered slimmers' bread

Lunch
175g/6oz fresh salmon steak, poached
75g/3oz canned button mushrooms heated in their own liquid
75g/3oz petits pois

Evening meal
1 packet Alveston Kitchens' Boeuf Bourguignon
75g/3oz haricots vertes
150g/5oz fresh strawberries, topped with half a 141g/5oz carton natural yogurt mixed with 15ml/1 tablespoon fresh orange juice

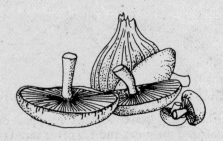

———— *Menu No. 4* ————

This menu includes a special evening meal cooked at home.

Drinks allowance:

Unlimited sugarless lemon tea, black coffee, water or slimmers' low-calorie drinks. Sorry, no milk allowed *but* see what we allow you with your evening meal (either before or after).

Breakfast

150ml/5 fl. oz unsweetened orange juice

Lunch

25g/1oz Edam cheese
1 eating apple
1 carton natural low-fat yogurt

Evening meal

2 pub measures gin or whisky (1/6gill/25ml) with low-calorie mixers
275ml/½ pint consommé
*Chicken Chasseur
75g/3oz Brussels sprouts
125g/4oz boiled potatoes
125g/4oz fruit salad, canned or fresh, topped with 30ml/2 tablespoons single cream

*Chicken Chasseur (2 servings)

To make the sauce, cook 50g/2oz chopped onion, 125g/4oz chopped tomatoes and 125g/4oz sliced mushrooms in a non-stick pan with a little water for 3 minutes. Add 2 glasses (225ml/8 fl. oz) dry white wine-

and season to taste. Grill without added fat 2 ×
225g/8oz chicken joints for 5 minutes, turning once to
brown both sides. Transfer the 2 chicken portions to a
pan, pour over the wine sauce, cover tightly and cook
gently for 30 minutes. Serve with the vegetables.

————————*Menu No. 5*————————

Another menu with an evening meal suitable for a special occasion.

Drinks allowance:

275ml/½ pint low-fat separated or skimmed milk for
drinks and cereal and as much sugarless tea and coffee
as you wish. As always there is no limit to the quantity
of water you can drink or for that matter to the number
of slimmers' low-calorie drinks, which you might find
useful if you cannot afford (calorie-wise) that extra glass
of wine which fellow diners might be having with their
meal.

Breakfast

25g/1oz All Bran, with milk from allowance

Lunch

Liver sausage salad made from 50g/2oz liver sausage,
unlimited lettuce, raw cauliflower, carrot, celery and radish
25g/1oz wholemeal bread spread with 7g/¼oz butter
1 orange

Evening meal

2 glasses dry sherry *or* 1 glass dry white wine
*Fish Veronique
125g/4oz potato, boiled in its jacket
75g/3oz carrots, boiled
125g/4oz broccoli, boiled
Apricot fool made from 25g/1oz dried apricots (soaked
overnight) blended with 150ml/5 fl. oz natural low-fat yogurt

*Fish Veronique (2 servings)

Poach or steam 2 x 175g/6oz fillets white fish. Top with a sauce made by thickening 275ml/½ pint fish stock with 2 rounded 5ml teaspoons cornflour; season to taste with salt, pepper and lemon juice. Garnish each fish fillet with 25g/1oz green grapes, halved, a lemon wedge, parsley and 1 tomato (can be grilled first).

-Vegetarian Menus-

Even vegetarians, whether just-can't-face meat or don't-think-it-in-the-world's interest to eat meat or strict Vegans, include slimmers. Although many vegetarians know a considerable amount about food values, they need and welcome help just like the rest of us when it comes to working out strict balanced 1000-calorie menus.

Slimming magazine's experts have seen to it that vegetarians can slim swiftly by using these menus. All the menus can be used by the vegetarian slimmer who never eats meat or fish or any products which involve killing an animal such as dripping, gelatine or suet, but who eats dairy products. Also included are one or two menus for the Vegan slimmer who never eats any animal products including dairy products at all.

——————*Menu No. 1*——————

Drinks allowance:

275ml/½ pint silver-top milk *or* 550ml/1 pint skimmed or separated milk, plus unlimited tea and coffee without sugar. Also as many hot Marmite drinks and low-calorie drinks and as much water as you like.

Breakfast

150ml/¼ pint unsweetened orange juice
25g/1oz 30% Bran Flakes
75ml/3 fl. oz milk (extra to allowance)
5ml/1 teaspoon sugar (optional)

Light meal

25g/1oz slice wholemeal bread scraped with low-fat spread
113g/4oz carton cottage cheese
watercress, tomato and stick of celery
125g/4oz black grapes

Main meal

*Stuffed pepper
125g/4oz carrots, boiled
125g/4oz cauliflower, boiled
1 McVitie or St Michael chocolate digestive biscuit

*Stuffed pepper (1 serving)

Cut 1 red or green pepper in half lengthwise; remove seeds and white pith. Cook 5ml/1 teaspoon chopped onion in 5ml/1 teaspoon corn oil. Add 50g/2oz flavoured Protoveg, reconstituted as directed, and 15g/½oz rice, boiled. Fill pepper with Protoveg stuffing and bake at 350°F, 180°C, gas Mark 4 for 20 minutes.

——— *Menu No. 2*———

Drinks allowance:

275ml/½ pint silver-top milk *or* 550ml/1 pint skimmed or separated milk, plus unlimited tea and coffee without sugar. Also as many hot Marmite drinks and slimmers' low-calorie drinks and as much water as you like.

Breakfast

141g/5oz carton low-fat natural yogurt mixed with 125g/4oz prunes, stewed without sugar, and 15ml/1 tablespoon unsweetened orange juice

Light meal

25g/1oz slice wholemeal bread
150g/5oz baked beans
2 eggs (size 4), poached

Main meal

½ grapefruit
198g/7oz can Appleford meatless curry
25g/1oz rice, boiled

———— *Menu No. 3*————

Drinks allowance:
275ml/½ pint silver-top milk *or* 550ml/1 pint skimmed or separated milk, plus unlimited tea and coffee without sugar. Also as many hot Marmite drinks and low-calorie drinks and as much water as you like.

Breakfast
25g/1oz slice wholemeal bread, toasted and spread with 50g/2oz curd cheese and a little Marmite

Light meal
* Egg Ratatouille
1 orange

Main meal
**Cheese and apple salad
141g/5oz carton low-fat natural yogurt with 5ml/1 rounded teaspoon honey

*Egg Ratatouille (1 serving)

Put 75g/3oz canned ratatouille in a small ovenproof dish. Break 2 eggs (size 4) on top, and season. Cover with foil and cook at 350°F, 180°C, gas Mark 4 for 25 minutes until eggs are set.

**Cheese and apple salad (1 serving)

Mix 1 stick celery, chopped, and a medium apple, sliced. Sprinkle with lemon juice and 2 chopped walnut halves. Stir in 15ml/1 tablespoon low-calorie cream-type salad dressing and 50g/2oz Edam cheese cut in cubes.

——— *Menu No. 4* ———

Drinks allowance:

275ml/½ pint silver-top milk *or* 550ml/1 pint skimmed or separated milk, plus unlimited tea and coffee without sugar. Also as many low-calorie drinks including Marmite as you like. Water is free!

Breakfast

25g/1oz All-Bran
75ml/3 fl. oz milk (extra to allowance)
1 orange

Light meal

*Coleslaw and blue cheese salad

Main meal

**Bean and tomato soup
Poached egg on spinach using 125g/4oz puréed spinach, 1 egg (size 4), poached and topped with 15g/½oz grated Edam cheese mixed with 15ml/1 tablespoon milk from allowance, then quickly browned under grill
½ small carton low-fat natural yogurt mixed with 1 small banana, sliced

*Coleslaw and blue cheese salad (1 serving)

Mix ½ a small carton of low-fat natural yogurt with 15ml/1 tablespoon lemon juice and seasoning to taste for the dressing. Shred 125g/4oz white cabbage, grate 1 carrot and finely dice 2 sticks of celery. Stir in the dressing and serve on a bed of lettuce, topped with 50g/2oz diced Danish Blue cheese.

**Bean and tomato soup (1 serving)

Fry 25g/1oz chopped onion and 1 peeled and chopped tomato in 5ml/1 teaspoon vegetable oil in a non-stick pan for 1 minute, stirring well. Add 200ml/7 fl. oz water or vegetable stock, bring to the boil, cover and simmer for 5 minutes. Stir in 65g/2½oz baked beans and 1.25ml/¼ teaspoon yeast extract. Liquidize in a blender or sieve, then reheat and season to taste. Serve sprinkled with chopped parsley.

———— *Menu No. 5* ————

Drinks allowance:

275ml/½ pint silver-top milk and as much sugarless tea and coffee as you wish. Also, unlimited low-calorie drinks and water.

Breakfast

150ml/¼ pint unsweetened orange juice
50g/2oz muesli with milk taken from allowance

Lunch

113g/4oz cottage cheese topped with ½ canned peach
large mixed salad (without dressing)

Evening meal

2 egg omelette with onion: melt 7g/¼oz butter or margarine in a non-stick pan and sauté 50g/2oz chopped onion. Pour in 2 eggs (size 4) already beaten with seasoning and a little water, and cook.
75g/3oz mushrooms, stewed in stock
1 tomato
75g/3oz boiled peas
fruit salad made with ½ apple, ½ orange, ½ grapefruit, ½ glacé cherry, 5ml/1 teaspoon lemon juice

Menu No. 6

For the Vegan slimmer (no animal or dairy products)

Drinks allowance:

40g/1½oz Granogen soya milk or Granolac, reconstituted as directed, for drinks throughout the day. Unlimited water and Marmite-type drinks.

Breakfast

½ grapefruit

25g/1oz muesli with Granogen or Granolac from allowance

Light meal

sandwich made from: 2 × 25g/1oz slices wholemeal bread
15g/½oz Granose sandwich spread
lettuce, watercress and cucumber slices
1 apple

Main meal

*Spaghetti savour

*Spaghetti savour (1 serving)

Boil 40g/1½oz spaghetti in lightly salted water until just tender. Drain. Chop 1 small onion and fry in 10ml/1 dessertspoon oil until just turning brown. Stir in 2.5ml/½ teaspoon curry powder, 45ml/3 tablespoons tomato juice, 2.5ml/½ teaspoon yeast extract, 10ml/1 dessertspoon peanut butter, 15g/½oz sultanas, 2.5ml/½ teaspoon grated lemon rind and 15ml/1 tablespoon lemon juice to make a smooth sauce. Stir in the cooked spaghetti and heat through. Serve piled on a plate, garnished with 15g/½oz salted peanuts, sprigs of watercress and a twist of lemon.

————*Menu No. 7*————

For the Vegan slimmer (no animal or dairy products)

Drinks allowance:
50g/2oz Granogen (soya milk) or Granolac, reconstituted as directed, for drinks throughout the day. Unlimited water and Marmite-type drinks.

Breakfast
1 Boots date and muesli bar
1 orange

Light meal
75g/3oz Nutbrown, Saviand or Sausalatas
large mixed salad of low-calorie vegetables (no dressing)

Main meal
*Vegetable curry
50g/2oz raw brown rice, boiled

*Vegetable curry(1 serving)

Peel and cut into large dices a selection of low-calorie vegetables, e.g. celery, mushrooms, courgettes, peppers, tomatoes, onions, carrots, cauliflower and 1 small cooking apple. Sauté together in 10ml/1 dessertspoon vegetable oil for 3-5 minutes. Stir in 5ml/1 level teaspoon curry powder and cook for a further minute, then stir in 5ml/1 teaspoon desiccated coconut, 15ml/1 tablespoon lemon juice and water just to cover the vegetables. Simmer until vegetables are tender. Serve with the boiled rice.

Eat plenty of low-calorie vegetables but don't dollop high-calorie butter on boiled vegetables or high-calorie mayonnaise on salad vegetables.

—Try-Something—
Different Menus

These 1000 calorie menus are for dieters who love to
cook or create attractive meals and who don't mind
spending some time preparing their meals.

Each menu includes at least one recipe. Although the
quantities given in the recipes are for one, you can easily
double or even quadruple the quantities to serve more
than one or freeze some portions for another day, but do
remember to eat only one portion yourself.

Having taken time to prepare your meals, sit down
and take your time to eat and enjoy it, since there is
evidence to show that food eaten slowly is more satisfying than food which is eaten quickly and 'on the move'.

———Menu No. 1———

Drinks allowance:
275ml/½ pint low-fat skimmed milk or reconstituted low-fat powdered milk, plus unlimited sugarless tea and coffee and slimmers' low-calorie drinks.

Fat allowance:
15g/½oz butter or margarine or 25g/1oz low-fat spread for spreading and cooking.

Breakfast
1 egg (size 3), boiled or poached
25g/1oz slice white or brown bread, lightly buttered

Lunch
*Vegetable casserole topped with cottage cheese
25g/1oz slice white or brown bread, lightly buttered
125g/4oz slice cantaloupe or yellow melon

Evening meal
150ml/¼ pint natural orange juice
2 chicken drumsticks (each 100g/3½oz raw), grilled
Boil 75g/3oz bean sprouts and 15g/½oz rice. Drain, mix together and serve grilled drumsticks on top
mixed green salad, without dressing

*Vegetable casserole topped with cottage cheese

Slice 175g/6oz aubergine, sprinkle with salt and leave to stand for 15 minutes. Wash and dry well. Slice 125g/4oz courgettes, 50g/2oz green pepper, 1 tomato and 50g/2oz onion. Dissolve 1 Bovril cube in 150ml/¼ pint boiling water. Layer vegetables in a small lightly greased casserole, ending with a layer of aubergine and seasoning between each layer. Pour stock over. Cover and bake at 350°F, 180°C, gas Mark 4 for 40 minutes. Uncover and spoon a small carton of cottage cheese with chives over the top. Return to oven for a further 10 minutes. Sprinkle with a little paprika pepper and serve.

When making casseroles do not pre-fry vegetables or meat in the traditional fashion. Simply cut up all the ingredients, put in casserole dish, pour a well-flavoured stock over, add a few herbs and cook until tender. If the meat was fatty, cool the casserole, skim off and discard fat, and then reheat.

Menu No. 2

Drinks allowance:
275ml/½ pint low-fat skimmed milk or reconstituted low-fat powdered milk. Unlimited sugarless tea and coffee and slimmers' low-calorie drinks.

Breakfast
50g/2oz mushrooms, poached in stock
2 rashers streaky bacon, crisply grilled
1 slice unbuttered slimmers' bread

Lunch
*Corned beef bake
75g/3oz peas

Evening meal
**Fish with almonds and tomatoes
75g/3oz broccoli
***Compote of pears

*Corned beef bake

Slice 75g/3oz corned beef into 3 slices. Peel and thickly slice a 150g/5oz potato. Place the corned beef in the bottom of a small oven proof dish. Cover with potato slices. Mix 30ml/1 rounded tablespoon Maggi French fried onion soup powder with 150ml/¼ pint water. Bring to the boil stirring, and simmer for 2 minutes. Pour over corned beef and potato. Cover and bake at 375°F, 190°C, gas Mark 5 for 35-40 minutes, or until the potato is tender.

**Fish with almonds and tomatoes

Grill 175g/6oz white fish with 3g/⅛oz butter. Top with 3g/⅛oz toasted flaked almonds and a wedge of lemon. Grill 2 large tomatoes cut in halves and sprinkled with chopped, fresh herbs. Serve fish with the tomatoes.

***Compote of pears

Peel, core and slice 2 pears. Bring 150ml/¼ pint water, 5ml/1 teaspoon brown sugar and 2 cloves to boiling point. Add the pears and 15ml/1 tablespoon sweet sherry and stew slowly until the pears are tender. Stir in 15g/½oz sultanas and serve hot.

Menu No. 3

Drinks allowance:

As much sugarless tea and coffee without milk, and as many low-calorie drinks and water as you like.

Breakfast

½ grapefruit without sugar
1 egg (size 4), poached
1 slice unbuttered slimmers' bread

Lunch

*Tuna bake
125g/4oz green beans

Evening meal

165g/5½oz raw pork chop, sprinkled with sage and crisply grilled
½ 64g/2¼oz packet Cadbury's Smash made up with 150ml/¼ pint water as directed; beat in 15ml/1 tablespoon milk and a little pepper. (Can be made into Duchesse potatoes and browned under grill)
75g/3oz peas
1 canned pineapple ring, drained
1 Lyons Maid Mini Brick vanilla ice cream
1 glacé cherry

*Tuna bake

Slice 1 tomato and place in the bottom of a small oven-proof casserole. Season. Flake 75g/3oz drained tuna fish and place on top. Slice a second tomato and use to cover the tuna. Season again. Sprinkle 25g/1oz grated Edam cheese over the top and bake in a moderate oven, 350°F, 180°C, gas Mark 4, for 20 minutes. Serve with green beans.

Menu No. 4

Drinks allowance:
275ml/½ pint low-fat skimmed or separated milk. Unlimited sugarless tea and coffee and low-calorie drinks.

Breakfast
2 rashers streaky bacon, well-grilled, served with 227g/8oz can tomatoes thickened with 5ml/1 level teaspoon flour and flavoured with Worcestershire sauce, 5ml/1 level teaspoon sugar, and salt and pepper
1 slice slimmers' bread

Lunch
113g/4oz carton cottage cheese with onions and pepper
large mixed salad
15ml/1 tablespoon low-calorie salad dressing
½ grapefruit topped with
15g/½oz mincemeat and grilled

Evening meal
*Chilli con carne
50g/2oz raw long-grain rice, boiled

*Chilli con carne

Fry 100g/4oz minced beef until brown and drain off the fat. Add 1 chopped small onion, 227g/8oz can tomatoes, salt and chilli powder to taste, 50g/2oz drained canned red kidney beans, 5ml/1 level teaspoon sugar, 5ml/1 level teaspoon flour. Heat to boiling point, stirring. Cover and simmer for about 1 hour. Serve with boiled rice.

—————*Menu No. 5*—————

Drinks allowance:
As much sugarless tea and coffee without milk and as many low-calorie drinks and water as you like.

Breakfast
2 rashers back bacon, well-grilled
5ml/1 teaspoon tomato sauce
1 slice slimmers' bread, unbuttered

Lunch
*Haddock and egg scramble
2 Energen crispbreads
1 apple

Evening meal
**Minced beef curry and accompaniments

*Haddock and egg scramble

Poach 100g/4oz smoked haddock in 60ml/4 tablespoons milk. Flake the fish in the milk. Add 1 egg (size 4), beaten with pepper to taste, and heat, stirring, until the egg is scrambled. Serve hot, sprinkled with chopped parsley.

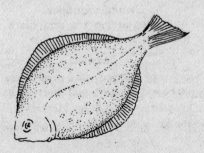

**Minced beef curry

Fry 100g/4oz minced beef in a saucepan for 5 minutes until browned. Drain off fat. Finely chop 25g/1oz onion, peel, core and finely chop 1 small (75g/3oz) apple, and grate 1 carrot. Add these with 7g/¼oz sultanas, 5ml/1 teaspoon concentrated curry sauce and 150ml/¼ pint water to the minced beef in the pan. Bring to the boil, stirring. Cover and simmer for 30 minutes. Boil 25g/1oz rice in salted water until tender. Drain and mix with 75g/3oz heated canned bean sprouts or lightly boiled fresh bean sprouts. Pour curried minced beef over and serve with 1 small sliced orange, 150g/5oz banana, sliced and tossed in lemon juice, 10ml/1 dessertspoon chutney, and 15g/½oz roasted peanuts.

─────── *Menu No. 6* ───────

Drinks allowance:

Unlimited sugarless lemon tea and black coffee and slimmers' low-calorie drinks.

Breakfast

25g/1oz Rice Krispies topped with a small banana, sliced, and served with 65ml/⅛ pint silver-top milk

Lunch

213g/7½oz Birds Eye beef stew with dumpling
75g/3oz Brussels sprouts

Evening meal
*Grilled mackerel with gooseberry sauce
231g/7½oz can Chesswood's button mushrooms
175g/6oz canned celery hearts
**Mincemeat, apple and orange salad
30ml/2 tablespoons top of the milk

*Grilled mackerel with gooseberry sauce

Wash and clean a 225g/8oz mackerel. Score the skin diagonally across two or three times on each side, season with salt and pepper and brush with oil. Grill for 5 minutes on each side. Purée 75g/3oz canned gooseberries with juice. Blend 2.5ml/½ level teaspoon arrowroot with a little cold water, stir into gooseberry purée and heat to boiling point. Simmer for 2 minutes and serve with grilled mackerel.

**Mincemeat, apple and orange salad

Heat together in a small saucepan 25g/1oz mincemeat and 60ml/4 tablespoons water. Peel and slice a 125g/4oz dessert apple and an orange. Stir into hot mincemeat sauce and continue to heat until the fruit is heated through. Serve hot.

Menu No. 7

Drinks allowance:
275ml/½ pint silver-top milk *or* 550ml/1 pint skimmed or separated milk. Unlimited tea and coffee (without sugar and using milk from allowance), low-calorie drinks and water.

Breakfast
2 rashers back bacon, well-grilled
50g/2oz mushrooms, poached in a little stock
1 crispbread, with a scraping of low-fat spread

Lunch
*Cheese and ham cocotte
1 crispbread, with a scraping of low-fat spread

Evening meal
125g/4oz slice honeydew melon
**Creamed kidneys
25g/1oz rice, boiled
75g/3oz broccoli, boiled

*Cheese and ham cocotte

Sauté 5ml/1 teaspoon chopped onion in 3g/⅛oz butter. Add 25g/1oz cooked ham, chopped, and 50g/2oz cottage cheese. Add salt, pepper and a pinch dried tarragon. Separate 1 egg (size 5) and add yolk to mixture. Whisk white until stiff; fold in carefully. Turn into a small ovenproof dish; bake at 375°F, 190°C, gas Mark 5 for 15 minutes until puffed and golden.

**Creamed kidneys

Pour boiling water over 2 lamb's kidneys; leave for 2 minutes. Drain kidneys; cut in quarters, discarding cores. Put kidneys in pan with 45ml/3 tablespoons beef stock, 50g/2oz mushrooms and 5ml/1 level teaspoon tomato purée. Cover, simmer gently for 20 minutes until tender. Blend 5ml/1 level teaspoon cornflour with a little water. Add to pan and bring to boil stirring continuously until sauce thickens. Add 15ml/1 tablespoon low-fat natural yogurt, and 1.25ml/¼ teaspoon prepared mustard and mix well. Serve with the rice and broccoli.

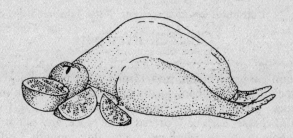

Menu No. 8

Drinks allowance:
275ml/½ pint silver-top milk or 550ml/1 pint skimmed or separated milk. Unlimited tea and coffee (without sugar and using milk from allowance), low-calorie drinks and water.

Breakfast
1 egg (size 4), poached
25g/1oz slice wholemeal or white bread, spread with 7g/¼oz butter

Lunch
*Chicken liver pâté
25g/1oz slice wholemeal or white bread, toasted
1 orange

Evening meal
**Haddock with olives
75g/3oz peas, boiled
***Banana surprise

*Chicken liver pâté

Put 50g/2oz chicken livers in small pan with 5ml/1 teaspoon chopped onion, and 15ml/1 tablespoon chicken
stock. Cover and cook gently for 10 minutes. Drain off
stock; place livers and onion in a bowl. Add 25g/1oz
curd cheese, dash of Worcestershire sauce, and salt and
pepper to season. Mash and pound until smooth. Chill.
Serve with the toast.

**Haddock with olives

Weigh out 7g/¼oz butter; use a little to grease an ovenproof dish. Place 175g/6oz haddock fillet in dish.
Sprinkle with salt, pepper and lemon juice. Skin and
chop 1 tomato; mix with 5ml/1 teaspoon chopped
onion, 2 stuffed olives, sliced, and 5ml/1 teaspoon
chopped parsley. Spoon this over the fish. Crush
15g/½oz 30% Bran Flakes and sprinkle on top; dot
with rest of butter. Bake 25 minutes at 375°F, 190°C,
gas Mark 5. Serve with peas.

***Banana surprise

Peel 1 small banana and place on a piece of foil. Sprinkle on 15ml/1 tablespoon orange juice. Fold up foil so no juice can escape. Place on baking sheet and bake for 20 minutes at 375°F, 190°C, gas Mark 5.

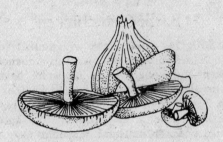

Menu No. 9

Drinks allowance:
275ml/½ pint silver-top milk *or* 550ml/1 pint skimmed or separated milk. Unlimited tea and coffee (without sugar and using milk from allowance), low-calorie drinks and water.

Breakfast
25g/1oz 30% Bran Flakes
75ml/3 fl. oz milk additional to drinks allowance
5ml/1 level teaspoon sugar (optional)

Lunch
*Coleslaw and ham salad

Evening meal
**Barbecued chicken
125g/4oz green beans, boiled
1 medium orange

*Coleslaw and ham salad

Mix 50g/2oz shredded white cabbage with 25g/1oz diced green pepper, 1 grated carrot, 1 stick celery, sliced, 50g/2oz ham, cut in strips. Toss in 30ml/2 tablespoons low-calorie cream-type salad dressing.

**Barbecued chicken

Sprinkle a 250g/9oz chicken joint with 5ml/1 level teaspoon flour. Heat 5ml/1 teaspoon oil in non-stick pan, add chicken and cook over a moderate heat until browned on all sides. Reduce heat; add 50g/2oz chopped onion, 75ml/3 fl. oz tomato juice, 10ml/2 teaspoons Worcestershire sauce, a few drops of soy sauce, and 2.5ml/½ teaspoon dry mustard. Season to taste. Cover pan; simmer for 45 minutes until chicken is tender. Baste the chicken with cooking liquid occasionally during cooking. Serve with green beans.

Menu No. 10

Drinks allowance:

275ml/½ pint silver-top milk for use in drinks; also unlimited sugarless tea and coffee, Bovril-type drinks and slimmers' low-calorie drinks.

Breakfast

1 egg (size 4), boiled
1 Ryvita crispbread, scraped with low-fat spread

Lunch

*Kebab on rice

Evening meal

**Lemony plaice rolls
125g/4oz potato boiled in jacket
125g/4oz mixed vegetables
1 orange with 142g/5oz carton natural low-fat yogurt

*Kebab on rice

Thread on a kebab skewer 50g/2oz lamb, diced, 1 kidney, cored and halved, 1 tomato halved, 25g/1oz green pepper cut into 4 pieces, and 4 button mushrooms. Brush with 5ml/1 teaspoon oil and grill, turning 3 or 4 times until the lamb and kidney are cooked, about 7 minutes. Boil 25g/1oz long-grain rice in lightly salted water. Drain and serve the kebab on the rice.

**Lemony plaice rolls

Defrost a 175g/6oz packet of plaice fillets. Sprinkle each fillet with pepper, lemon juice and a little chopped parsley. Roll up and secure with wooden cocktail sticks. Cook between 2 plates over pan of boiling water until tender, 10-15 minutes.

Menu No. 11

Drinks allowance:

Unlimited sugarless lemon tea and coffee without milk and unlimited slimmers' low-calorie drinks and water.

Breakfast

25g/1oz All-Bran
75ml/3 fl. oz silver-top milk
1 orange

Lunch

1 small carton cottage cheese with onions and pepper
2 digestive biscuits
1 medium banana

Evening meal

*Beef olive
75g/3oz runner beans
75g/3oz cauliflower
**Peach Melba

*Beef olive

Flatten a thin 150g/5oz slice of braising steak. Season with salt and pepper and rub with a clove of garlic, if liked. Chop 25g/1oz lean boiled ham and mix with 15ml/1 tablespoon grated carrot, 15ml/1 tablespoon chopped onion, 10ml/2 teaspoons tomato purée, salt and pepper, and a pinch of mixed herbs. Moisten with 15ml/1 tablespoon beef stock. Spread the mixture over the piece of steak, roll it up and tie with thin string or cotton. Put 15ml/1 tablespoon each of chopped onion and grated carrot into a small ovenproof dish. Place the beef olive on top. Add 125ml/4 fl. oz beef stock and a pinch of mixed herbs. Cover and bake at 325°F, 170°C, gas Mark 3 for 1 hour or until the meat is tender. Serve with runner beans and cauliflower.

**Peach Melba

Crush or sieve 50g/2oz raspberries and sweeten to taste, if necessary, with artificial liquid or powdered sweetener. Skin 1 fresh peach, cut in half and remove the stone. Place the 2 peach halves on 50g/2oz vanilla ice cream and top with the sieved or crushed raspberries.

When stewing fresh or dried fruit save calories by using a low-calorie liquid or powdered sweetener if you need to sweeten the fruit. Always add it after stewing.

Menu No. 12

Drinks allowance:

275ml/½ pint silver-top milk for use in drinks, also unlimited sugarless tea and coffee, Marmite, Bovril and slimmers' low-calorie drinks.

Breakfast

½ grapefruit
1 slice slimmers' bread, toasted and scraped with low-fat spread
5ml/1 teaspoon marmalade or jam

Lunch

150g/5oz ham steak, grilled without fat
1 ring of canned pineapple
1 tomato, grilled
75g/3oz sweetcorn
1 apple, orange or pear

Evening meal

*Spanish omelette with prawns
salad of lettuce, cucumber and watercress (no dressing)
125g/4oz green grapes

*Spanish omelette with prawns

Heat 7g/¼oz butter in a non-stick frying pan. Add 1 skinned and chopped tomato, 25g/1oz chopped onion, and 25g/1oz diced green pepper, and fry gently until soft. Beat 2 eggs (size 4) together with 30ml/2 tablespoons water and seasoning. Pour into the pan and cook until set. Turn out onto a plate, top with 50g/2oz shelled prawns, and serve with salad.

——Menu No. 13——

Drinks allowance:

275ml/½ pint low-fat skimmed milk or reconstituted low-fat powdered milk. Unlimited sugarless tea and coffee and slimmers' low-calorie drinks.

Breakfast

125ml/4 fl. oz natural orange juice
1 large thin slice bread or toast, lightly buttered (7g/¼oz maximum)

Lunch

*Kidneys in oxtail sauce
125g/4oz green beans
1 apple

Dinner

175g/6oz turkey breast, grilled
salad made from 1 carton mustard and cress, 1 tomato,
50g/2oz fresh or canned sweetcorn and 50g/2oz green pepper
125g/4oz black grapes

*Kidneys in oxtail sauce

Melt 3g/⅛oz butter or margarine in a small pan. Wash 2 lamb's kidneys; remove skin and cores, then slice. Fry kidneys gently in the melted fat to seal the surfaces. Stir in 156g/5½oz can condensed oxtail soup with 30ml/2 tablespoons water and 5ml/1 teaspoon Worcestershire sauce. Simmer gently for 15 minutes. Serve hot, sprinkled with chopped parsley.

———Menu No. 14———

Drinks allowance:
275ml/½ pint silver-top milk and as much sugarless tea and coffee and as many low-calorie drinks as you wish.

Breakfast
½ grapefruit topped with 1 heaped 5ml teaspoon of mincemeat. Grill for 3 minutes

Lunch
*Baked sole and pineapple
75g/3oz cooked spinach
75g/3oz boiled carrots
1 apple, orange or pear

Evening meal
*Chicken Sauté *Espagnole*
75g/3oz boiled peas
225g/8oz boiled cauliflower
1 Birds Eye lemon and orange or chocolate mousse

*Baked sole and pineapple

Place 225g/8oz fillets of sole in an ovenproof dish, sprinkle well with lemon juice, salt and freshly milled pepper. Cover with foil and bake in warm oven, 325°F, 170°C, gas Mark 3 for 15 minutes. Slice 125g/4oz fresh pineapple and arrange in an ovenproof serving dish. Place the fillets of sole on the top and return to oven for 6 minutes.

*Chicken Sauté *Espagnole* (2 servings)

Heat 10ml/1 dessertspoon oil in a sauté pan and brown 2 chicken joints (225g/8oz raw weight) on all sides; remove and keep warm. Chop 1 onion and 1 clove garlic finely, add to pan and cook until soft. Add 50ml/2 fl. oz dry sherry, raise heat for a few seconds to reduce by half, then add 5ml/1 teaspoon tomato purée and 150ml/¼ pint chicken stock. Put the chicken joints back in the pan, season to taste, cover and simmer gently until tender – about 40 minutes. Meanwhile, skin 3 tomatoes, cut in quarters and remove seeds. Place the chicken joints in a hot dish. Strain the sauce and thicken with 5ml/1 level teaspoon cornflour. Return to sauté pan with the tomatoes and simmer for 1 minute. Spoon the sauce over the chicken and serve.

−Calorie Counter−

Calories per 25g and 1oz unless otherwise stated

	Calories per 25g	per 1oz
Almonds, shelled	141	170
Anchovies	35	40
Apples, eating or cooking	9	10
Apricots, fresh	6	7
Apricots, dried	45	52
Arrowroot	88	100
Asparagus, boiled	2	3
Aubergine, raw	4	4
Avocados	56	64
Bacon		
back rashers, raw	107	122
streaky rashers, raw	103	118
back rashers, fried	116	133
streaky rashers, fried	124	142
back rashers, grilled	101	116
streaky rashers, grilled	105	120
gammon rashers, grilled	57	65
gammon joint, boiled, lean meat only	42	48
Baking powder	41	47

	Calories per 25g	per 1oz
Bananas, with skin	12	13
Barley, pearl, dry	90	102
Beans		
French, boiled	2	2
runner, boiled	5	5
broad, boiled	12	14
butter, boiled	24	27
haricot, boiled	23	27
baked, canned in tomato sauce	16	18
kidney, raw	85	97
lima, raw	31	35
soya	109	125
Bean sprouts	7	8
Beef		
brisket, boiled	81	93
mince, raw	55	63
rump steak, raw	49	56
rump steak, grilled, lean only	42	48
sirloin, raw	68	78
sirloin, roast, lean only	48	55
stewing steak, raw	44	50
stewing steak, stewed	56	64
Beetroot, boiled	11	13
Blackberries, raw	7	8
Blackcurrants, fresh	7	8
Black pudding, fried	76	87
Brains, calf and lamb, raw	27	31
Bran	52	59
Brazil nuts, shelled	155	177
Bread		
white	58	67
Hovis	57	65
wholemeal	54	62
currant	62	71
malt	62	71

	Calories	
	per 25g	per 1oz
soda	66	75
bread rolls (all kinds)	72	83
chapatis, made with fat	84	96
chapatis, made without fat	50	58
Broccoli, boiled	4	5
Brussels sprouts, boiled	4	5
Butter	185	211
Cabbage		
raw	5	6
boiled	4	4
Carrots		
raw	6	7
boiled	5	5
Cashew nuts, shelled	156	178
Cassava, fresh	39	44
Cauliflower, boiled	2	3
Caviar	65	74
Celeriac, boiled	4	4
Celery		
raw	2	2
boiled	1	2
Cheese		
Camembert	75	86
Cheddar	101	116
Danish Blue	89	101
Edam	76	88
Parmesan	102	116
Stilton	115	132
cottage	24	27
cream	110	125
processed	78	89
cheese spread	70	80
Cherries, fresh, with stones	10	12
Chestnuts, shelled	43	49

	Calories per 25g	per 1oz
Chicken		
raw, meat only	30	35
roast, meat only	37	42
roast, on bone	25	29
Chicory, fresh	2	3
Chocolate, milk or plain	132	160
Clams, raw in shells	13	15
Cob nuts (hazelnuts), shelled	95	108
Cockles, without shells	12	14
Cocoa powder	78	89
Coconut, fresh	88	100
Coconut, desiccated	151	173
Coconut, milk	5	6
Cod		
fresh or frozen fillets, raw	19	22
frozen steaks	17	19
grilled steaks	24	27
poached fillets	23	27
Coffee, instant, dry	25	28
Coley, raw, on bone	18	21
Corn oil	225	257
Corned beef	54	62
Cornflour	89	100
Courgettes, raw	3	3
Crab, meat only, boiled	32	36
Cranberries, fresh or frozen, raw	4	4
Cream		
single	53	60
double	112	127
whipping	83	95
sterilized, canned	57	66
Cucumber	3	3
Currants	61	69
Curry powder	58	67
Custard powder	89	100

| | Calories | |
	per 25g	per 1oz
Damsons, with stones	9	10
Dates, with stones	53	61
Dripping, beef	223	255
Duck		
roast, meat only	47	54
roast, meat, fat and skin	85	97
Eel		
stewed	50	57
smoked	38	43
Eggs		
white only	9	10
yolk only	85	97
whole egg, size 1		95
whole egg, size 2		90
whole egg, size 3		80
whole egg, size 4		75
whole egg, size 5		70
whole egg, size 6		60
Figs fresh	10	12
dried	53	61
Flour		
white	88	100
wholemeal	80	94
cassava	86	98
rye (100 per cent)	84	96
soya, full fat	112	128
yam	80	91
Garlic	2	2
Gelatine	84	96
Ghee	205	237

	Calories per 25g	per 1oz
Ginger		
ground	65	74
stem	70	80
Goose, roast	80	91
Gooseberries		
fresh, ripe dessert	9	11
fresh, cooking	4	5
Grapefruit		
flesh only	6	6
with skin	3	3
juice, unsweetened	8	9
Grapes		
black	13	15
green	15	17
Greengages, stewed without sugar, plus stones	9	11
Haddock		
raw, on bone	18	21
fried, on bone	40	46
smoked, steamed, on bone	16	19
Hake		
raw, on bone	19	22
raw, fillet	18	21
steamed, fillet	26	30
Halibut		
raw, on bone	23	26
steamed, on bone	33	37
Ham, boiled, lean only	54	62
Hare		
stewed, meat only	48	55
stewed, on bone	35	40
Hazelnuts, shelled	95	108
Heart		
pig's, raw	23	26

	Calories	
	per 25g	*per 1oz*
lamb's, raw	30	34
ox, raw	27	31
Herring		
raw	58	67
grilled, on bone	34	39
Herring roes, soft, raw	20	23
Honey	72	82
Ice cream, vanilla	42	48
Jam (and marmalade)	65	75
Kidney		
lamb's and pig's, raw	22	26
ox, raw	21	24
Kippers, baked, on bone	28	32
Lamb		
lean leg, roast	48	54
lean loin chop, grilled,		
on bone	30	35
lean shoulder, roast	49	56
lean cutlets, grilled,		
on bone	24	28
lean stewing, cooked, on bone	32	37
Lard	223	255
Leeks		
raw	8	9
boiled	6	7
Lemon, juice	2	2
Lemon sole, raw, on bone	20	23
Lentils		
raw	76	87
boiled	25	28
Lettuce, raw	3	3

	Calories per 25g	per 1oz
Liver		
calves', raw	38	44
calves', fried	63	72
chicken, raw	34	38
chicken, fried	48	55
pig's, raw	38	44
lamb's, raw	48	51
ox, raw	41	46
Lobster		
boiled, with shell	10	12
boiled, meat only	30	34
Loganberries, fresh	4	5
Low-fat spread	91	105
Luncheon meat	78	89
Lychees, raw	16	18
Macaroni		
raw	93	106
boiled	29	33
Mackerel		
raw	56	64
fried, on bones	34	39
Maize, whole grain	91	104
Mandarins, canned	14	16
Mango, raw	15	17
Margarine	182	208
Marrow, boiled	2	2
Marzipan	111	127
Melon		
canteloupe, weighed with skin	4	4
yellow, honeydew, weighed with skin	3	4
watermelon, weighed with skin	3	3
Milk (per 550ml/1 pint)		
pasteurised or silver top		370

	Calories	
	per 25g	per 1oz
Channel Island or gold top		490
homogenized, red top		370
goat's		400
fresh, skimmed milk		190
dried skimmed milk	89	100
evaporated milk, whole	40	45
consensed milk, whole, sweetened	80	92
Mincemeat	59	67
Mulberries, raw	9	10
Mushrooms		
raw	3	4
fried	53	60
Mussels, without shells	22	25
Mustard and cress	3	3
Mustard, dry	113	129
Nectarine, with stone	12	13
Noodles, boiled	31	35
Oatmeal, raw	100	113
Octopus, raw	18	21
Olive oil	225	257
Olives, in brine, with stones	20	23
Onions		
raw	6	7
fried	86	98
Oranges		
with skin	7	7
flesh only	9	10
juice, unsweetened	10	11
Oxtail, stewed, on bone	23	26
Oysters		
raw, with shells	2	2
raw, without shells	13	15

| | Calories | |
	per 25g	per 1oz
Parsley	5	6
Parsnips		
raw	12	14
boiled	14	16
roast	28	32
Partridge, roast, on bone	32	36
Pastry		
choux, raw	54	61
choux, baked	83	94
flaky, raw	107	122
flaky, baked	141	161
shortcrust, raw	114	130
shortcrust, baked	132	150
Peach, fresh, with stone	8	9
Peanuts, fresh (shelled)		
and roasted and salted	143	163
Pears	7	8
Peas		
raw	17	19
boiled	13	15
Peppers, red or green	4	4
Pheasant, roast, on bone	34	38
Pilchards, canned in tomato sauce	32	36
Pineapples, fresh	12	13
Pistachio nuts, shelled	157	179
Plaice		
raw, on bone	23	26
steamed	23	26
Plums, fresh, with stones	9	10
Pomegranate, flesh only	11	13
Pork		
roast, lean meat	46	53
roast, lean and fat	71	82
chops, grilled, lean meat,		
on bone	33	38

	Calories per 25g	per 1oz
chops, grilled, lean and fat, on bone	64	74
Potatoes		
old, raw	22	25
boiled	20	23
baked, weighed with skins, no butter	21	24
chips	63	72
roast	39	45
instant mash, made up, no milk or butter	18	20
crisps	133	152
Prawns, without shells	27	30
Prunes		
dried	40	46
stewed, without sugar	18	21
Pumpkin, raw	4	4
Rabbit		
raw	31	35
stewed, on bone	23	26
Radishes	4	4
Raisins	62	70
Raspberries, fresh or frozen	6	7
Redcurrants, fresh	5	6
Rhubarb		
fresh	2	2
stewed without sugar	2	2
Rice		
raw	90	102
boiled	31	35
Sago	89	101
Salmon		
raw	46	52
canned	39	44

	Calories	
	per 25g	per 1oz
smoked	36	41
steamed, weighed with bones and skin	40	46
Sardines		
canned in oil, fish plus oil	83	95
canned in oil, fish only	54	62
canned in tomato sauce	44	51
Sausages		
beef, raw	75	85
beef, fried	67	77
beef, grilled	66	76
pork, raw	92	105
pork, fried	79	91
pork, grilled	80	91
Scallops, steamed, without shells	26	30
Scampi, fried, with breadcrumbs	79	90
Semolina, raw	88	100
Shrimps, without shells	29	33
Snails, flesh only	23	26
Sole		
raw	20	23
steamed, weighed with bones and skin	16	18
Spaghetti		
raw	95	103
boiled	29	33
Spinach, boiled	8	9
Spring greens, boiled	3	3
Spring onions	9	10
Strawberries, fresh or frozen	7	7
Suet, shredded	206	236
Sugar, white or brown	98	112
Sultanas	63	71
Sunflower seed oil	225	257
Swede, boiled	5	5

	Calories	
	per 25g	per 1oz

Sweetbreads		
lamb, raw	33	37
lamb, fried	57	66
Sweetcorn		
fresh or frozen , raw	32	36
boiled	31	35
Syrup, golden	74	85
Tangerines, with skin	6	7
Tapioca, raw	90	103
Tomatoes, raw	4	4
Tomato juice, canned	4	5
Tongue, sheep or ox, boiled	72	83
Treacle, black	64	73
Tripe, stewed	25	28
Trout, steamed, on bone	22	25
Tuna		
canned in oil, fish plus oil	72	83
canned in oil, fish only	52	59
Turkey		
raw, meat only	27	30
roast, meat only	35	40
Turnips, boiled	4	4
Veal		
cutlet, coated in egg and		
breadcrumbs, fried	54	61
fillet, raw	27	31
fillet, roast	57	66
Vegetable oils	225	257
Venison, roast, meat only	49	56
Vinegar	1	1
Walnuts, shelled	131	150
Watercress	4	4

| | Calories | |
	per 25g	per 1oz
Wheatgerm	88	101
Whelks, boiled, without shells	23	26
Whitebait, fried	131	150
Whiting		
fried, on bone	43	49
steamed, on bone	16	18
Winkles, boiled, without shells	18	21
Yeast, baker's, fresh	13	15
Yogurt, low-fat, natural	13	15

Index